D0319926

Wooden Spoon

Rugby's charity supporting disadvantaged children and young people

WOODEN SPOON
RUGBYWORLD'06

Editor
Ian Robertson

Photographs

Getty Images
and Fotosport UK

Queen Anne Press

A QUEEN ANNE PRESS BOOK

© Lennard Associates Limited 2005

First published in 2005 by
Queen Anne Press, a division of
Lennard Associates Limited
Mackerye End
Harpenden, Herts AL5 5DR

All rights reserved. No part of this publication may be reproduced, stored in a retrieval system, or transmitted in any form or by any means, without the prior permission in writing of the publisher, nor be otherwise circulated in any form of binding or cover other than that in which it is published without a similar condition including this condition being imposed on the subsequent purchaser.

A catalogue entry is available from the British Library

ISBN 1 85291 663 X (hardback)
ISBN 1 85291 664 8 (paperback)

Production Editor: Chris Marshall
Cover Design/Design Consultant: Paul Cooper
Printed and bound in Slovenia

The publishers would like to thank Getty Images and Fotosport UK for providing most of the photographs for this book.

The publishers would also like to thank Empics, Inphopics and Chris Thau for additional material.

TRUE PASSION

TRAVIS PERKINS IS THE UK'S LEADING SUPPLIER OF TIMBER, BUILDING MATERIALS, PLUMBING & HEATING AND TOOL HIRE.

BUILDERS MERCHANT
AWARDS
EXCELLENCE
2004

NATIONAL
BUILDERS
MERCHANT
OF THE YEAR

2004

PROUD SPONSORS OF
NORTHAMPTON SAINTS

Travis Perkins

www.travisperkins.co.uk

Contents

Rugby crazy?

We're mad about it too!

That's why we're the official energy partner to England Rugby and sponsor of the Powergen Cup.

But our support doesn't stop there. Our National Rugby Community Programme is the largest of its kind in the world reaching over 400.000 people each season.

From the champions of today to the champions of tomorrow, we're giving everyone the chance to go rugby crazy!

powergen.co.uk

Positive Energy

FOREWORD

by HRH THE PRINCESS ROYAL

BUCKINGHAM PALACE

HRH The Princess Royal
Royal Patron
of Wooden Spoon

It gives me great pleasure to report that Wooden Spoon continued to grow at an impressive pace in 2005. In the last year, the charity has pledged its 10 millionth pound in over 20 years of service to a Dublin-based charity. This is a particularly fitting gift given the origins of Wooden Spoon.

The membership of Wooden Spoon expands on a daily basis. Social membership of the charity now stands at 10,000 supporters, and it is hoped that membership will reach its goal of 20,000 in the next two years. Anyone who has a love of the game and the willingness to help disadvantaged and disabled children should consider joining.

In the past 12 months, Wooden Spoon has pledged funds to over 50 new projects supporting disadvantaged children and young people. This is more than the sum total of the projects supported in the charity's first decade. I warmly congratulate the trustees, staff, volunteers and many supporters of the charity without whom this remarkable sustained growth would not have been possible.

Anne

Wooden Spoon

Rugby's charity supporting disadvantaged children and young people

These Charming Men: Jack and Willie John by TRACEY LARCOMBE

Royal Patron: HRH The Princess Royal
Patrons: Rugby Football Union • Scottish Rugby Union
                 Welsh Rugby Union • Irish Rugby Football Union

ABOVE Legends of Ireland rugby Jack Kyle, Willie John McBride, Syd Millar and Mike Gibson, accompanied by Billy Trimble, Lee Mulholland and Laura-Jayne Kerr, at the Annual Ulster Dinner.

FACING PAGE Peter Spratt and Colin Anderson from the AndersonSprattGroup presenting a cheque from the first sailing event of One Squadron, with joint Honorary Presidents Dr Jack Kyle and Willie John McBride OBE and Honorary Secretary Jimmy Burns.

*T*he first thing that strikes me upon meeting Willie John McBride is not just the way he comes bounding down the hotel steps like a 25-year-old as opposed to someone who's not long turned 65; it's the sheer size of the man … he's HUGE. He grasps my hand in an all-encompassing shake that suggests it may never see the light of day again, and leads me to where fellow Irish rugby legend Jack Kyle is sitting in the hotel bar.

I have managed to shoehorn some time into their busy schedules (Jack's daughter regularly complains that his social diary is far more full and exciting than her own) to talk about, well, everything really. From the British and Irish Lions tour they went on in the summer, to their past careers, their thoughts on professional rugby, to finding out more about the Northern Ireland branch of Wooden Spoon; so I was in for a busy time of it. I also got a little more information than I bargained for.

It was some time, several cups of coffee and a lot of laughs later before the two of them deigned to disclose that not only was the place they had chosen for us to meet in Belfast the most bombed hotel in the world ('You won't believe the amount of times the windows have been replaced in here!') but also, and perhaps more alarmingly, neither of them is quite who he says he is.

WJ Well, you see, I'm not Willie John at all … actually I'm William James … this Willie John thing came from around where I was born – there were a lot of Willie Johns and as I was 'W.J. McBride' in the newspapers when selection was announced, everybody assumed I was Willie John and it just stuck.

JK And I'm not Jack Kyle, really … I was christened John, but everyone just called me Jackie.

Of course with chaps as charming and legendary as these, one can forgive the choice of hotel … but THEIR NAMES? Given that these two are among the most recognised names in rugby history it comes as a bit of a shock and, funnily enough, they didn't know each other's real names until this point either. But despite being firm friends now, during their playing years their paths rarely crossed – as Kyle's career was coming to an end, McBride's was just beginning. Then they both got involved with Wooden Spoon and not only forged a lasting bond between them but a solid foundation for the charity in Northern Ireland.

JK Being of different eras altogether we never really played together or travelled together or anything like that. And with me being abroad most of my life really, we hadn't very much contact until I got back. And I suddenly found myself a co-chairman of the Wooden Spoon – I don't even know how that happened!

WJ It's a great thing though, because we have a small committee but a very active one, with a lot of contacts, but then that's Wooden Spoon. But it's a marvellous charity for a number of reasons; it's about making these kids' lives a bit better. We've both been lucky, as a lot of people in rugby are, in that we have a lot of friendships and we've done well in life, and it's nice to give back a bit of time. Of course the other thing is it's about fun, it's about people getting together and having fun as well as raising money. I like that about it, and the other thing I like about it is that if you raise some money, Spoon doubles it – that is a big attraction, and it's spent here and people will support that.

JK Also, of course, there are guys like Colin Anderson, who formed 'The Yacht Squadron' …

WJ Oh yes, we raised £17,000 in one afternoon! Colin is in advertising and PR and he's got a big yacht and a lot of friends who have yachts, so he came up with the idea of getting 15 yachts together and inviting guests for £100 each for the day. We sailed around Strangford Lough and then all went to a place called the Port Ferry Arms, which is a big fresh fish restaurant, and had lunch. And everything on the table was out of Strangford Lough. What a spread! It was unbelievable. You get someone like Colin Anderson to do that; I mean, Jack, that must have cost him thousands!

Then of course we have the Ulster Supporters Club at Ravenhill, and they've come up with quite a bit of money, so the charity is pretty healthy here and we're certainly proud of it. It's also moving into the provinces … I went to Coleraine, which is further northwest; I was at a dinner there and I couldn't believe the number of Wooden Spoon ties! So it is spreading.

For McBride the coming together of the provinces in the name of charity is perhaps even more poignant, particularly because of the years during the troubles when rugby kept people together, and players from the North and South of the country were united as one team. But away from sport there were many dark days when friends and colleagues were lost.

WJ One of the great things about rugby here through those years was that it stood steadfast; there

AND MAKE ROOM FOR SPORTS

SO YOU CAN SPREAD OUT

BUSINESSELITE HAS NO MIDDLE SEAT

delta.com/uk

For further information on our BusinessElite® service
from London and Manchester to the U.S., please call 0800 414 767 or visit our website.

ABOVE Jack Kyle and Willie John McBride with children and a teacher from the Longstone Riding School for the Disabled in Armagh.

were no games cancelled. These clubs and people went out of their way to make sure that was the case and I think that's a great plus for the game of rugby, particularly because of what was going on.

I got caught up in Bloody Friday when there were 26 bombs ... I didn't know where to run. They weren't nice days ... some people have forgotten about those days; I haven't forgotten. I lost friends, like my friend John Holdy. I opened his new business down there in the docks, I spent the afternoon with him and had a great laugh and two days later they shot him dead for no reason. And they said it was a mistake but he was still dead. I will never forget that. I sometimes wonder what people like him would have been doing now.

JK The good thing was that the rugby was played among all Ireland, unlike the divide in soccer, and never at any time did a Southern side fail to travel to the Northern side or vice versa, and I think that was a wonderful thing.

Thankfully, over the course of time things have moved on in Northern Ireland – the only reason we can sit happily in the Europa Hotel without feeling incredibly nervous. And of course, so much has changed in rugby, too. When Kyle and McBride were selected for an international or Lions team the only way they heard about it was by reading it in the newspaper, and when they did go on tour a large amount of time was spent just getting there and back.

JK For the Lions tour to New Zealand in 1950 we went out by ship. From Liverpool, across the Atlantic, through the Panama Canal and across the Pacific. It took us just over a month to get to Wellington. We had 30 players and two staff, neither of whom were rugby coaches; there were no coaches then as the captain of the side coached the team. There were a couple of PT trainers on board and we'd do our training up on the deck – we'd run all the way around the deck thinking 'How long do we have to do this before it's half a mile or a mile!' We spent three months in New Zealand and played something like 23 or 24 games; we had a month in Australia, then it took us another month or so to come back.

WJ Mine was a little bit more modern because I went in 1962 and we went by plane, but the plane in those days flew over land as much as possible so you were refuelling all the time and it seemed like it took about three days to get there. But if you can imagine you're the size of us – it took about three more days to unfold after sitting in this thing for so long! My first tour to South Africa was around four and a half months, I think; but the difference then was that we took rugby to every little corner of the country when we were there.

Listening to the two reminisce it's clear the most recent tour was very different to those Jack and Willie John experienced. It's also obvious that with the onset of the professional era some of the more traditional aspects of a Lions tour have changed quite significantly.

WJ They were wonderful days; it was all about people. There was some hassle this time about players having their own rooms; they didn't share rooms. On our tours, every three or four days you went to a different place and shared a room with a different person, so you got to know everybody during the tour. Someone asked me when we were in Racine recently what happened if you shared a room with somebody you didn't like. I said, well we kept them in there until they did! That's how we had to build a team.

JK One of the things they said when we got on the ship at Liverpool was look guys you've all got your own friends from your own countries but when you come down to a table you take the first available seat. You don't sit down and wait for your friends – you get to know the guys, and this was one of the great things of the tour.

WJ Rugby is the greatest team game, and when it comes to a Test match it's about the little precision things that happen. Knowing that your team-mate is on your right or your left. On this tour the first Test team didn't play together at all; none of the Test teams played together except in the Test. You can't expect to go out and beat the All Blacks like that. A lot of things in life and certainly in rugby are about confidence, and if you have a team that lacks confidence going on to that field they're going to be beaten, because you must believe in your heart of hearts that you're going to win, and I don't think they did.

JK The thing most of us who were players felt sorry for was that the chaps just weren't getting games. You've got to have the opportunity – one or two games is not enough on a Lions tour to show what you can do with such a big group of players. I would like to see Lions tours extended with more games because the small towns look forward to it so much and it's a wonderful experience for players.

WJ I also didn't feel like there were key people to build the team around. There was no Martin Johnson, let's put it that way, and when things were going wrong there, no one that people could look to and say 'What do we do?' I think in general there were mistakes made and it's easy to be critical, but I just hope someone sits down to see where this tour went wrong and puts the lessons learnt on paper so it doesn't happen again. The Lions are over 100 years old and they have stood the test of time. There's nowhere else in sport where four countries and cultures come together to create a team; it's a special thing and it will continue to be.

Many things have changed since 'their day' and they are quick to point out this is not necessarily a bad thing – it's just different. For them rugby came second to the importance of

LEFT Skipper Willie John McBride in action during the Lions' unbeaten tour of South Africa in 1974.

FACING PAGE Jack Kyle kicks for touch against England.

having a career, and in this area the two couldn't have been further apart. Jack qualified as a doctor and went on to be a surgeon in Sumatra and Zambia from 1962 to 2000, while Willie John worked for the Northern Bank after leaving school and stayed there until he retired in 1994.

JK I spent 35 years in Zambia as a full-time surgeon in a smallish town with a very big catchment area around it. When I went out there, I was the only surgeon in my town and the next so you had to become a jack of all trades … someone suddenly presented you with something and you had to go back to the books. A friend of mine used to say, 'You'll have no trouble with this operation, Jack. Just get out your surgery manual and read it up!' There was a consoling factor in a way that if you didn't do it there was nobody else – for the Zambian people there was no option for them and they were basically very grateful for what we did. It was a terrific experience.

WJ My father died very young and I was brought up on a farm with my mother; my two elder brothers were in farming and I went into banking. The Northern Bank were super and really supportive. I could never have done it had they not been so good. I suppose they got their pound of flesh back in later years, but I did something like 36 years in banking and I really enjoyed it.

JK Rugby was a small part of our lives back then compared with our careers, and because our parents were brought up during the Depression years it was very important to have a job. You never know what's going to happen on the rugby field, and if you leave it till you've finished and you want to go to university then you're a lot older than everyone else there. So my advice to lads today would be get into your career because with a bit of luck you've got a lot of life after rugby to live.

I would defy anyone to not be affected by the enthusiasm and humour of these two men, talking about their experiences in rugby and in life. The overwhelming impression I have when I (reluctantly) have to leave their company is how much they have gained from rugby, the difference it made to their lives and how much it still means to them today.

JK Back in the old days we used to listen to the alikadoos and they used to say 'Well, the game's important but it's the friends that will last you …' and we used to say 'Oh, here they go again!' But when you're our age you realise, especially for me being away for so long and coming back and meeting all my friends again. I often wonder what life would have been like if I hadn't been involved in rugby and I think it wouldn't have been anything like as interesting, or as good.

WJ When I first started playing the game as a young man, you were always guided by your elders. It was about teaching discipline on the rugby field, it was about respect for one another, building teamwork, how to live with one another. It was about developing young men for the world of work, working in a team, and understanding people – that's what it was all about, and we came back from those tours richer men. I probably learnt more on a rugby tour than I ever did at work about how to get on with people, how to get the best out of people, and indeed in leadership. That's why we played rugby and I sometimes wonder today if we have forgotten about all that … it wasn't all about money. Fair enough, it's a way of life now, but I think we must hold on to some of the old traditions if this game is to survive.

REACH
FOR THE BEST

It's rare to find a recruitment consultancy who tackle personnel requirements with such tenacity and unfailing dedication. An unrivalled approach that has enabled Pertemps to remain unchallenged at the top of the league as the UK's leading independent recruitment consultancy.

As market leaders, we have developed our reputation not just by "filling positions" but by adding value to our client portfolio, a philosophy which is reflected in the diverse range of leading blue-chip companies that currently utilise our services.

Operating in three service divisions: commercial and professional, industrial and driving and technical and executive, our fully integrated service ensures that we are able to deliver quality personnel with the right skills, in the right place at the right time.

So, if you are seeking to win the competition for business, make sure that you retain the competition for talent by choosing Jobs@Pertemps, Britain's most successful independent recruitment consultancy.

JOBS
@PERTEMPS

Head Office: Meriden Hall, Main Road, Meriden, Warwickshire CV7 7PT.
Tel: 01676 525000. Fax: 01676 525009
www.jobsatpertemps.co.uk
An equal opportunities employer

COMMENT
& FEATURES

Ars Prima Regni Posse Te Invidiam Pati

by PAUL STEPHENS

'While our thoughts throughout the summer have been with the Lions, there are matters of greater import to be considered, all of which will affect the domestic game and require management of the highest order.'

It was said that good armies marched on full stomachs, though whoever coined that aphorism probably suffered from perpetual malnourishment syndrome. The food maxim isn't entirely misplaced, as General Friedrich Paulus found to his cost at the battle of Stalingrad during Operation Barbarossa, where many of his beleaguered infantry starved to death. The greater verity is that successful armies triumph because they are well led. The best armies possess the best leaders. Those who fail are invariably poorly managed. So it is in business, just as it is in sport.

Soon after the tumultuous end of the Zurich Premiership season in England, the British and Irish Lions left Heathrow for New Zealand. This would be the best prepared Lions in history intoned their head coach, Sir Clive Woodward. This nugatory nonsense is now Woodward's sporting epitaph. The leadership shown by the over-praised Woodward was disastrous. This is no clever view with the benefit of hindsight. It was clear well before the massively overblown party set off that Woodward's Delphic optimism was hugely misplaced, the preposterous appointment of Alastair Campbell to oversee media relations being only one of Woodward's catastrophic misjudgments. The wonder was that Woodward, with his boundless self-belief, didn't call on Carole Caplin as the Lions' lifestyle guru and Delia Smith to be head cheerleader.

While Woodward quite rightly has to shoulder most of the blame for what was a hugely disappointing, and largely futile, exercise, one wonders why he was allowed so much unfettered freedom to do as he pleased when assembling his elephantine group, who, he predicted, would be the first Lions to return victorious from the Land of the Long White Cloud since John Dawes's troops did so in 1971. Why did no one on the Lions' committee urge restraint? After all, was not this the same wacky Woodward who presided over at least three of England's Six Nations Grand Slam failures? Not to mention the embarrassing 1999 World Cup quarter-final defeat by South Africa in Paris, when he chose Paul Grayson ahead of Jonny Wilkinson to wear the number 10 shirt. Did Woodward not say 'Judge me on my record' after the 1999 World Cup? He sure did.

For those who chose to stay at home rather then witness live the witless Lions stumble from one calamity to another, there is some consolation. Never again will a television audience be obliged to behold Woodward's unapologetic smirk when being interviewed, as he attempts to explain away another international rugby defeat. He was lauded as the apparent mastermind of England's World Cup triumph in 2003, though as one of the all-time great Lions, Willie John McBride, said of that campaign: 'Clive Woodward didn't win the World Cup for England, nor did Jonny Wilkinson. It was Martin Johnson's exceptional leadership that was the difference. Woodward was fortunate to have him in his side.' Wasn't he just.

The 2005 Lions are now history, though they will be judged as among the poorest in their glorious antiquity. If Woodward had been in charge of a public company instead of so publicly making an ass of himself, the shareholders would have booted him out by now, his next expedition being a trip to the job centre. He will be remembered as the Arthur Balfour of international rugby management. Balfour, by some distance, was the least effective Tory prime minister of the last century; at least until John Major took office.

While our thoughts throughout the summer have been with the Lions, there are matters of greater import to be considered, all of which will affect the domestic game and require management of the highest order. It is far too early to say whether the omens are genuinely propitious or otherwise, though sooner rather than later decisions will have to be made to determine whether the Premiership will continue in its present form, albeit with new sponsors Guinness.

What is to be done about the frictional trend of growing antipathy towards and lack of respect for referees, which has led England's elite referees' manager, Colin High, to lament the ponderous pace of recruitment and the development of those displaying the necessities to adjudicate at the highest level? 'Unless we can see some improvement soon,' said High recently, 'we may have to look overseas to get properly qualified referees to take charge of some Premiership games.' And this is before the Rugby Football Union come to terms with the dwindling numbers of referees coming into the game at more junior levels; or take stock of the creeping influence of agents, drug issues, player indiscipline, and the seemingly limitless number of overseas players plying their trade in the Premiership.

The last four of those topics are a mirror of what besets the Barclays Premier League in football. But in that game there is no equivocation about promotion and relegation. It is sacrosanct, as many believe it should be at the top of the club rugby pile in England; though for how much longer in the oval-balled game is anybody's guess.

One thing is incontestable: the immediate past season would not have been anything like as interesting, indeed exciting, as it was without the vital promotion and relegation battle bearing upon it. The club season in England – with only Leicester of the top dozen making any significant impact in the Heineken Cup – would have been buried weeks earlier, while we all waited for the Premiership final, had there not been an almighty scrap involving Worcester, Northampton, Harlequins, Leeds and London Irish, one of whom was destined for relegation, depending on the outcome of the very last round of matches. What a frenzied Saturday that was, with all six games kicking

BELOW Sir Clive Woodward and his media adviser, Alastair Campbell, face the press in an unavailing attempt to explain away another defeat on the 2005 British and Irish Lions' tour to New Zealand.

off at the same time, and Harlequins losing out and being consigned to at least one season in National One. With a new grandstand under construction at The Stoop, there was some incongruity in this, given that Quins' chief executive, Mark Evans, is most vociferous in his support of ring-fencing the Premiership. 'How can you invest in a business when the future is so uncertain and you lose most of your central funding once relegated?' asks Evans. Well plenty of hopeful investors do, as those holding shares in Marconi, Railtrack or Jarvis will testify.

While reflecting on West Bromwich Albion's great escape, Alan Hansen could have been talking rugby when he said: 'The big winner was the afternoon itself. The elation, twists and turns, the intense drama. It was a great day for English football.' So it was for rugby's Premiership.

Back in April there was drama of an entirely different sort, when the grassroots clubs ignored the advice of the game's hierarchy, including Fran Cotton and Bill Beaumont, and voted at a special meeting in London for Martyn Thomas rather than Jack Rowell to be the next chairman of the RFU. Thomas, the time-served council member for Notts, Lincs and Derbys, replaces Graeme Cattermole, who resigned last November after a period of bitter infighting. Some thought that Rowell, with his mix of a rugby and business background, would make the best candidate, but Thomas emerged successful by 403 votes to 290 on the back of his campaign theme of 'one game, one union'. Now he must live up to it.

The danger were Rowell to have been elected could well have been that the Premiership clubs would be allowed to take more powers to themselves. This almost inevitably would have led to the end of the promotion and relegation argument in favour of a closed shop. The clubs could then

demand that they have the final say in the appointment of referees for Premiership games. Player discipline could be under their control, as might all broadcasting negotiations and rights. Surely, we have seen how supine the Football Association has become in dealing with the major clubs and how that troubled organisation's ability to mete out punishments which reflect the gravity of the offence in disciplinary matters has weakened in the face of opposition from the rich and powerful who have the wherewithal to employ the best lawyers. Do we want this sort of depressing scenario to develop in our game? Are we going to accept without question that the hysterical bullying and foul-mouthed hectoring of referees, which is standard behaviour in football, is to become an inevitable concomitant in rugby?

If Thomas gets his way there seems little likelihood of this happening. 'Ideally,' asserts Thomas, 'my vision is for a successful England, with a vibrant Premiership, supported by strong community clubs. Before we achieve this there are some fundamental issues, which have to be resolved. I can see things from the Premiership clubs' perspective. It's in their interest to own and manage their affairs for the benefit of their shareholders and we have to turn their difficulties with the RFU's management ambitions into positives.

ABOVE Worcester players and supporters celebrate Drew Hickey's try in the final match of the season, against Northampton Saints at Sixways, which helped the Warriors retain their Premiership status.

RIGHT Chief Executive Mark Evans seeks consolation from below, as Harlequins are relegated from the Premiership and drop into National One.

OVERLEAF Martyn Thomas, the newly-elected chairman of the Rugby Football Union, has some hard decisions to make, some of which might be unpopular with certain elements in the game.

'But my first duty is to help deliver a successful England. For this to happen, the Premiership clubs have to nurture and bring on players who are qualified to play for England. Equally, an international coach needs those players for longer periods than has been the case, to develop a style of rugby, which will give Andy Robinson a chance of putting together a side capable of winning the next World Cup. Before then we must look at the problems of overplaying our England players. As it stands, a player is allowed 32 games a season; and anything over 40 minutes constitutes a game. What some clubs are doing to get round this regulation is to allow a player to stay on the field for 39 minutes, which doesn't count as a game. This is nonsense.'

Thomas is similarly forthright about other contentious issues, though he is strong in his belief that an accommodation can be reached with the clubs. 'It is fundamental that we have automatic promotion and relegation,' contends Thomas. 'There is a long-form agreement in place, which runs to June 2008, and any club seeking to change the one-up, one-down arrangement would have to seek the consent of the RFU before any variation could be made. Play-offs are a compromise, and the National One clubs don't want them anyway.

'There is a determination at the RFU not to cover over our problems with any more sticking plaster,' avers Thomas. 'We must be resolute. We can see how not to do it by looking at soccer, and we're not going to go down that road.'

Thomas faces some hard decisions. Unless he is going to attempt to be all things to all people, there is the real risk that he will be shunned in some quarters. If that is the price to be paid for advancing the cause of England rugby, so be it. Let him draw comfort from the words of Seneca: *Ars prima regni posse te invidiam pati*. The first qualification of a ruler is the ability to endure unpopularity.

Warren Gatland
from Wasps to Where?

by CHRIS JONES

'That memorable semi-final was Gatland's first trip to the ground since his sacking and while he resisted the urge to do a lap of honour throwing 'V' signs at his former employers, his players ensured a huge feeling of satisfaction.'

Ask Warren Gatland to pick his favourite moment from three trophy-laden years as London Wasps director of rugby and a mischievous smile instantly breaks out. His memory races back to the Wasps dressing room under the ageing main stand at Lansdowne Road in Dublin in the moments after the team had defeated favourites Munster in the 2004 Heineken Cup semi-final. The visitors' dressing room door is flung open and the corridors are filled with the sound of

ABOVE Warren Gatland has returned home to New Zealand after nearly ten years working in Europe. In 2005 he took over as coach to the Waikato NPC side.

Wasps players singing 'There's only one Warren Gatland'. They kept that up seemingly for ages until their point had been made, and it was one Gatland appreciated deeply.

Three years earlier, the political movers and shakers of Irish rugby had masterminded Gatland's sacking as national coach, installing local boy Eddie O'Sullivan. It was the lowest period of Gatland's rugby life and he vowed never to be in that position again.

That memorable semi-final was Gatland's first trip to the ground since his sacking and while he resisted the urge to do a lap of honour throwing 'V' signs at his former employers, his players ensured a huge feeling of satisfaction. That is why he decided to quit as London Wasps director of rugby on the eve of a third successive English title, having also won the Heineken Cup and the Parker Pen Challenge Cup. Gatland went at a time of his choosing – something Irish rugby chiefs never allowed him to do.

Gatland, whose final Wasps match was fittingly that successful Zurich Premiership final against Leicester at Twickenham in May, remembers the Munster match as if it were yesterday. He says: 'It was a hugely emotional day and it was a kind of payback for what had happened with the Ireland job. To be honest, when they threw open the dressing room door and sang at the top of their voices "There's only one Warren Gatland" it was pretty embarrassing.

'Before the Munster semi-final, Lawrence [Dallaglio] spoke to the players and said "Those bastards got rid of Warren. Let's shove it down their throats," and I didn't have to say anything. I was just looking to get out of the dressing room because it was getting so emotional. Getting to so many finals with Wasps – winning the English title three times and doing the double with the Heineken Cup in 2004 against Toulouse at Twickenham – is why you are involved with the sport. You want to experience those big days out.'

Gatland has returned to his beloved Waikato with his wife and two children, and has gone back a changed man. Having spent nearly ten years away from home as a Kiwi coach plying his trade in Europe, Gatland has broadened his horizons and seriously improved his rugby CV at the same time. He will be a strong candidate to take over from Graham Henry as All Blacks coach after the 2007 World Cup and acknowledges the debt he owes to Wasps and men like Dallaglio and head coach Shaun Edwards.

In turn, they make it abundantly clear that it was Gatland – who took over Wasps when they were at the bottom of the Premiership – who put the structure in place to allow the club to become

PROUD SPONSORS OF

RIGHT Signing off in some style. Gatland with Wasps skipper Lawrence Dallaglio after the club's third Zurich Premiership final success in as many years.

champions of Europe. The support systems for the players are now being copied by other clubs and Gatland admits to having been in charge of a rugby 'orphanage' at Wasps, where problem players were nurtured and made to feel part of a family club.

Matt Dawson, the England scrum half, has blossomed following his move to Wasps from Northampton and he believes the challenging environment created by Gatland and Edwards is responsible for his improved form and recall to England and Lions colours. Gatland explains: 'Shaun often says we have become an orphanage for problem players and we seem to be able to bring something extra out of those guys. This is a great club and it will always have a special place in my heart.

'In New Zealand we believe that rugby is our game and we own it. That's why the All Blacks have been so successful in the past, but the game is

BEEN CONVERTED?

ABBOT ALE

ON WASPS AND LAWRENCE DALLAGLIO

now so global and my eyes have been opened by being able to coach over here. I have learnt a hell of a lot and I am taking it back with me.'

It is Waikato in the National Provincial Championship who will immediately benefit from Gatland's enlarged rugby knowledge base, but there is also the small matter of building a new home on a plot of land he has bought near Hamilton. Then there will be a technical role with the Chiefs in the newly expanded Super 14 tournament – a natural next step for the former Waikato hooker. From then on it will be about how the New Zealand Rugby Football Union decide to use his obvious talents.

Given his outstanding rugby CV, this is a rugby expert that his fellow countrymen will have to utilise, or else he may just head back over the equator. The English triple league champions have a saying 'Once a Wasp, always a Wasp', and Gatland says it with real pride.

BELOW Gatland poses in front of the Waikato logo. With his rugby pedigree, the former Wasps coach must be a strong candidate to succeed Graham Henry after RWC 2007.

Wallaby Scrappers
Phil Waugh and George Smith

by RAECHELLE EDWARDS

'Along with New Zealand's Richie McCaw, Waugh and Smith have changed the way the game is played. They're not only out and out hard at the tackle contest, stealing the ball, they have a "complete" game …'

Eddie Jones is a lucky man. He has two special ingredients that ensure the Wallabies are consistently successful – outstanding flankers who win the ball at the tackle contest time and again.

'Phil Waugh and George Smith are enormously important because they are world-class players,' Jones says. 'Bob Dwyer has this expression that to be a top side in the world you need five world-class players and they're definitely in that category.'

BELOW George Smith and back-row partner Phil Waugh (with wristband) lead a Wallaby break against the All Blacks at Sydney in the 2003 Tri-Nations.

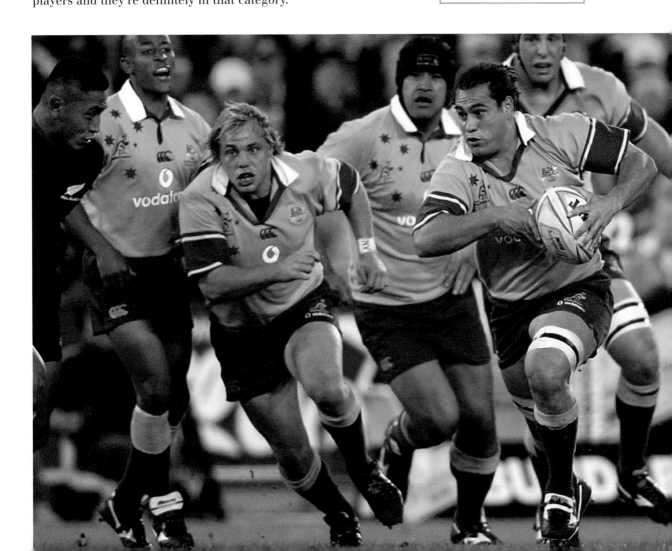

RIGHT No quarter given. Phil Waugh, on Waratah duty, charges fellow Wallaby George Gregan of the Brumbies during the sides' 2005 Super 12 clash at Canberra Stadium.

Along with New Zealand's Richie McCaw, Waugh and Smith have changed the way the game is played. They're not only out and out hard at the tackle contest, stealing the ball, they have a 'complete' game – they are fit, fast, strong, competitive, intuitive, powerful in defence, solid ball runners and have good passes.

Jones has a constant dilemma about which one of these 25-year-olds to play at open-side. 'We've got two blokes whose best position is definitely seven, but we can't play both of them so over the last couple of years we've played George at six and Waughy at seven and that's worked really well for us.

'You'd wish you could use them in their best position to greater effect, but then I'd have to play one for 50 minutes and one for 30 minutes; I think it's more effective for both of them to play for 80 and one in a different position.'

Phil Waugh is competitive and a leader. These attributes will stand him in good stead for a long and successful international rugby career. Jones describes Waugh's style as 'abrasive' and says he's a good reader of the game, analytical and makes a contribution to the way the Wallabies play. Waugh sees his own assets as his speed and physical strength. To be a successful open-side breakaway you need to be able to pilfer ball, and Waugh is a specialist. 'That comes with reading the game, seeing the opportunity and seizing it ... being in the right place at the right time,' he explains.

Waugh first played rugby, on Sydney's Northern Beaches, when he was four years old. He progressed smoothly from junior regional rugby to school level, playing in the 1st XV for the prestigious Shore School and captaining the Australian Schoolboys side in 1997. He then went on to play for Australia's oldest rugby club, Sydney University, where he had a year in the colts team, at the same time representing Australian U19 and then captaining Australian U21 in 2000. He progressed to Sydney University first grade, debuted for the Waratahs in 1999 and played his first Test match in 2000.

He's had a dream run in rugby, but Waugh could have chosen to pursue another sport, having excelled at cricket as a wicket-keeper and batsman. He played three years in his school's 1st XI and captained the Greater Public Schools combined team.

On the field Waugh is energetic. Off the field he is two years through a business degree at the University of Sydney, which he is committed to completing; he hopes to have a career in business when he retires.

A recent new father to son Jack, Waugh has had an exciting year, with the New South Wales Waratahs reaching their first Super 12 final in the history of the competition. Waugh's openly competitive nature and intensity were a key contributing factor to the team's turnaround. He puts it down to playing a smarter style of rugby and winning the tight games.

His position in world rugby was noted with a place in the southern hemisphere team for the IRB 'Rebuilding after the Tsunami' Rugby Aid match at Twickenham in March 2005. 'That was a great experience – one of the most memorable weeks in my career so far,' Waugh says.

Growing up, Waugh idolised Michael Jones from New Zealand and Wallaby breakaway David Wilson. 'I still admire those guys and what they achieved in rugby and now it's a matter of making sure I achieve in rugby,' he says.

Waugh has had his fair share of accolades. He was named the Australian Super 12 player of the year in 2001 and received the John Eales Medal in 2003 for the Wallabies' best and fairest player, an award decided by the votes of the Wallaby players themselves.

Waugh counts the 2003 World Cup as his greatest career highlight, even though the Wallabies failed to topple England in the final. Their victory in the semi-final against the All Blacks in front of his home crowd was particularly exciting. Waugh has a strong Kiwi connection, as his uncle Laly Haddon is one of the most-capped New Zealand Maori.

Waugh, like any great player, is critical of his own game and feels that the rivalry with Smith keeps him motivated. 'While there's pressure there's always that expectation to perform and knowing that if I don't perform George will be ahead of me,' he says. Waugh feels that having Smith as a competitor has made him a better player, 'and I dare say the same for him … we are often pushing each other to new levels and I think that improves both our games'.

Smith agrees: 'It's healthy. We push each other to the limits and that's what you want in an opposition flanker to make you a better player and I think that's what we do for each other … if we can keep on doing that our games can both improve.'

Eddie Jones describes Smith as 'unique'. 'He's got the uncanny ability to be able to find the ball and he's able to bob up in different situations and find links between the backs and forwards and different parts of our attack,' explains the Wallaby coach.

Smith is ten months younger than Waugh and is also soon to be a first-time dad. His father is Australian and his mother is Tongan. He has five brothers and two sisters. His dad introduced him to rugby when he was four years of age, and like Waugh he played where he grew up, around the Northern Beaches of Sydney.

Smith has always played for the Manly club, in juniors, colts and then first grade. He also progressed through the age groups in the Australian teams, playing in the U16 in 1996, Australian Schoolboys in 1997 and 1998, Australian U19 in 1999, Australian U21 in 2000, before debuting for the ACT Brumbies and the Wallabies that same year.

Smith's big break came in 1999, when he played half a game of club rugby for Manly against Penrith that Eddie Jones and Ewen McKenzie happened to be watching. 'We signed him [for the Brumbies] … because he had that unique ability to find the ball,' says Jones. 'At that stage of his career he was very much someone who just attacked the ball at the breakdown. I think now he's developed a much stronger game … George doesn't come across as competitive, he comes across as pretty laid back but on the field he's a pretty fierce competitor.'

Playing for the Brumbies has been a critical part of Smith's development as a player. He learnt a great deal from fellow ACT back-rowers Owen Finegan and Jimmy Williams and from Toutai Kefu when they played together for the Wallabies. He is a good-natured person and says the toughest opponents he has faced are McCaw, Waugh and Kefu.

To play at the highest level as a flanker, Smith feels that you have to push the limits

LEFT Phil Waugh, having received the John Eales Medal 2003 from the former Australia captain.

FACING PAGE George Smith celebrates the series defeat of the 2001 Lions on his 21st birthday.

– 'if you can do that and play to the edge of the law I think you are doing your job, as long as you're not giving away penalties,' he says.

Along with Waugh, Smith has redefined the role of a flanker at the tackle contest, which has led to countless turnovers in favour of the teams he represents. 'You do play on instinct ... I have a big advantage in that I'm a lot shorter than some other players in opposition teams and my reaction to the ball is a lot quicker,' he explains.

But there is much more to Smith's game than sniffing out the ball. He describes how his style of play has evolved. 'In the early years as a professional footy player I was definitely a scavenger, I followed the ball around everywhere and tried to make a nuisance of myself at the breakdown ... I think I've improved my ball-running ability and defensive abilities around the field.'

Smith is creative in attack; he is good at organising the forwards and at times plays like a second fly half. Smith counts winning the third Test against the British Lions in 2001 to secure the series on his 21st birthday as a 'huge highlight' in his career. He has also won the coveted John Eales Medal, in its inaugural year of 2002; and in 2001, 2003, 2004 and 2005 he was voted the Brett Robinson Players' Player at the Brumbies. Smith says these accolades mean a great deal as they are awarded on the basis of votes cast by his fellow players.

A rarity for the professional era, Smith is rarely injured. In this year's Super 12 tournament he missed a game with an AC (acromioclavicular) joint injury having played more than 60 consecutive matches. 'I

think I'm lucky, I seem to be at the bottom of every ruck and seem to get smashed a fair bit in every game,' he comments. He is dedicated to rehabilitation and recovery between every game.

Neither Waugh nor Smith played in the Wallaby World Cup victory in 1999, but they both played in Australia's 2003 campaign to defend the Webb Ellis Cup, and while they reached the final both are hungry to win 'Bill' back in 2007. The Wallabies are already preparing for that World Cup, to be held in France, and Waugh and Smith will be senior members of the team.

'You go into a World Cup wanting to win it and if you don't win it, you've failed the goal you set, so there's no secret that come 2007 Australia is going to be wanting to win the World Cup,' Waugh says. 'There are plenty of contributing factors [to winning the tournament] ... it's a matter of performing well in the big games during the World Cup.'

Eddie Jones feels the contribution of Waugh and Smith will be instrumental in France. 'They should be at their optimum playing age by then ... they'll be 27 and players generally reach their maximum physical development around 27 or 28,' he explains. 'They'll still have young bodies with great experience ... if their form, fitness and desire keep where they are at the moment they'll be very influential players.'

Refereeing: A Point of View

by CHRIS JONES with DAVID McHUGH

"'When we talk about the breakdown we have to accept the fact that players have to stay on their feet but it's not an automatic offence if a player does go off his feet.'"

David McHugh, the specialist refereeing adviser to the British and Irish Lions on the 2005 New Zealand tour, knows better than most the real truth about the so-called differences in whistle-blowing either side of the equator.

It seems to be a fact of rugby life that whoever is in the 'other' hemisphere on tour has to deal with a new way of refereeing. The Lions were no different, talking about different interpretations, particularly at the breakdown, that left them bemused and penalised.

Thankfully, head coach Sir Clive Woodward had asked the vastly experienced McHugh, who officiated in three Rugby World Cups and two European finals, to be part of the management team

in New Zealand. Limerick-born McHugh was able to cut through the red tape and get straight to the officials taking charge of Lions matches.

So, is there such a gulf between referees in the north and south? 'There is a difference in perception rather than fact as you can see from the statistics from the last World Cup which show very little between the officials from the two hemispheres,' said McHugh. 'This is very significant.'

World Cup official statistics back up his conclusion, with the number of penalties, time of ball in play, points etc showing hardly any difference. However, one area which the two hemispheres continue to debate is the breakdown, as we saw on the Lions tour.

McHugh said: 'When we talk about the breakdown we have to accept the fact that players have to stay on their feet but it's not an automatic offence if a player does go off his feet. This could be for a number of innocent factors and I don't agree that southern hemisphere referees and those from the north differ hugely in their attitude to this area of the game.

'However, there is a difference in interpretation and judgment in applying the laws at the breakdown. The IB gives a ruling on a law and then it is down to the individual unions how they decide to operate with the rule. There is no doubt that Super 12 has come out with statements to try

ABOVE All Black Richie McCaw nails France's Cédric Heymans. As long as McCaw regains his feet after the tackle, he can play the ball, whichever side of it he finds himself.

FACING PAGE David McHugh on duty in the 2002-03 Heineken Cup match between Neath and Leicester at The Gnoll.

and change the way a referee officiates to get closer to Test rugby because the Super 12 countries were at a disadvantage at the last World Cup.

'It is also a fact that 40 to 50 per cent of penalties occur at the tackle area and that's true for the northern and southern hemisphere. It's not particular to one half of the globe. What Richie McCaw and Marty Holah are doing at the breakdown is legal because they get straight back up on their feet after making the tackle and it doesn't matter – in law – if they are on the "wrong side" of the ball because that's legal and they can play it.

'There are a lot of factors why New Zealand players are so good in this area and their concentration on sevens is one that should be acknowledged. We have players like Brian O'Driscoll who can do exactly the same thing at the tackle, but we would prefer centres not to be involved in the breakdown as it takes them out of the midfield play once the ball is recycled.

'It's all about being at the tackle situation before a ruck has been called. Once more than two people are involved then the referee will call "ruck", and the on-the-ground contest should then finish.'

Other areas also cause irritation, and it has appeared for some time that the forward-pass ruling has become very inconsistent. McHugh has a simple formula that he believes can help and

explained: 'We have seen a lot of discussion about forward-pass rulings and I take a law of physics approach to this area of the game. It isn't a forward pass if the player giving the pass is moving forward, keeping running after offloading. I think it is probably fair to say that ERC [European Rugby Cup] refereeing of competitions in the northern hemisphere is closer to Test rugby than the Super 12 tournament.

'In the Super 12 tournament you didn't see as many players committed to the breakdown, but it is more of a contest in this area of the game at international level and that is what we saw on the 2005 Lions tour.

'I took charge of an Australian Test with Argentina in Buenos Aires some years ago and the Wallaby coach Rod Macqueen asked me about some decisions after the match, and I told him "This isn't Super 12", and he accepted my point of view. He recognised that was the case.'

The use of new technology is a key development for officials in charge of matches and McHugh has definite views on this aspect of the game. Increasingly, referees go to the video referee when a try is scored because they know the storm that could result from a bad call when they didn't use all the available help. 'One of the most used words in the game is "stakeholder", and there is no doubt that television and sponsors are massive stakeholders in the game,' he said.

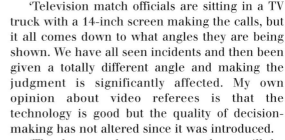

'Television match officials are sitting in a TV truck with a 14-inch screen making the calls, but it all comes down to what angles they are being shown. We have all seen incidents and then been given a totally different angle and making the judgment is significantly affected. My own opinion about video referees is that the technology is good but the quality of decision-making has not altered since it was introduced.

'The human element means there will be different interpretations. I have been a video referee and you can have your hands behind your head until the ball gets into the 22 and then as it gets within five metres you have to be ready for action. To be honest, I don't recall any major howlers by referees, so you could ask: why was the video ref brought in?

'I am neither for it or against it. On the subject of touch judges and their input to the referee, I would ask this question. Why do you need the touch judge to call offside in the backs when he is 40 to 50 metres away from the breakdown?

'The referee is one metre away and can see exactly when the ball is out and is able to look up and make a call on offside. How can the touch judge rule when the ball has actually come out of the ruck?

'The whole modus operandi has changed because of the introduction of new technology and it's not necessarily for the better. Technology should be there to help.'

LEFT The video referee was called in after Martin Corry crossed for the Lions v Taranaki on the 2005 tour, in case his foot had been in touch. On technology, McHugh opines: '[It] is good but the quality of decision-making has not altered since it was introduced.'

The Lions Caged
the 2005 Tour to New Zealand
by CHRIS HEWETT

'Sir Clive Woodward, unpredictable in his approach and unapologetic in his embrace of innovation, selected the most populous squad in the annals of rugby touring.'

The biggest squad, the most lavish support – medical, logistical, tactical, financial, you name it – and, sadly, the greatest rugby disappointment of our age. Even the New Zealanders were disappointed, and they won the Test series three-zip. The British and Irish Lions had been no strangers to heavy defeats in All Black territory down the years; the 1966 and 1983 vintages had both been whitewashed in four-match rubbers, failures that left their captains, Mike Campbell-Lamerton and Ciaran Fitzgerald, scrambling to defend what little was left of their sporting reputations. But this was worse, somehow. This was desperate.

Maybe the shock should not have been so great. Certainly, a cold-eyed assessment of the 2005 Lions' prospects before the 45-strong party (42, actually, owing to the late departures of Stephen Jones, Gareth Thomas and Jason Robinson) left Heathrow in late May would have thrown up three very good reasons why the tourists might struggle to make an impact.

For a start, there was the history of the thing – and as far as the All Blacks are concerned, history is very definitely not bunk. They had not lost in Auckland, the venue for the final Test, since France beat them in injury time with the 'try from the ends of the earth' in 1994. Eleven years. Ridiculous. Even worse, their record in the South Island, where the Lions were scheduled to open their account in Christchurch, bordered on the petrifying. On only 13 occasions in the 101 years of Test rugby in the Land of the Long White Cloud had the silver-ferned hordes failed to win there. Thirteen failures, including draws, in more than 90 contests.

Secondly, there were the All Blacks in the here and now. They had fairly marmalised the French in Paris in the last Test of their 2004 autumn trek around the capitals of Europe; the Canterbury Crusaders had won yet another Super 12 title playing some blinding rugby in the process; and in the pre-

RIGHT Wellington, second Test: Daniel Carter pops the ball past Lions full back Josh Lewsey and chases it down to score his first try of a match that featured a remarkable personal performance from the All Black fly half.

Lions preparatory Test against Fiji, the national team had posted 90-plus points. Their familiar players – the Richie McCaws, the Daniel Carters, the Tana Umagas – looked in the very finest fettle; the relative unknowns – the Rico Gears, the Sitiveni Sivivatus – looked exceptional. With Steve Hansen and Wayne Smith growing into their roles as Graham Henry's right and left hands, the word 'daunting' was never far from the lips.

And lastly? The Lions themselves. Sir Clive Woodward, unpredictable in his approach and unapologetic in his embrace of innovation, selected the most populous squad in the annals of rugby touring. Yet try as he might, he could not bridge the gap between quantity and quality. Four years previously in Australia, the Lions had travelled with Keith Wood at hooker and Phil Vickery at tight-head prop, Scott Quinnell at No. 8 and Rob Howley at scrum half. Above all, they had Martin Johnson of Leicester and the world. The 2005 squad did not have a Wood or a Vickery, still less a Howley, and nothing even approaching a Johnson. They did not even have a Quinnell once Lawrence Dallaglio was invalided out of the proceedings less than half an hour into the opening match with Bay of Plenty in Rotorua.

ABOVE Lawrence Dallaglio lies injured, his tour ended after less than 30 minutes of the opening match against Bay of Plenty.

FACING PAGE All Black lock Ali Williams touches down for New Zealand's opening try in their 21-3 first Test victory on a drenching night in Christchurch.

What was more, they did not have a Jonny Wilkinson, a Jason Robinson or a Richard Hill. Not, at any rate, as we had come to know them in their prime. Robinson, struggling with a persistent knee injury, had not enjoyed the most prosperous of seasons, and that lack of prosperity continued in New Zealand to the extent that he was half the man he had been in 2001. Every other inch a world-class player, you might say. Both Wilkinson and Hill had recovered from more serious knee conditions just in time to make the trip, which suggested they had compromised on their rehabilitation programmes. Sure enough, neither appeared fully fit; sure enough, both saw their tours curtailed as they attempted to play at Test pitch and were found wanting.

None of these negatives could be placed at Woodward's door. It was not his fault that New Zealand was the most hellish place in the world to win a Test series. Nor was it his fault that Henry's fleet-footed All Blacks were well on the way to developing a new, high-impact style of rugby based on solid set-piece work, furious intensity at the breakdown, deep-angled support running, supremely efficient passing out of contact and the maximisation of space, each and every element put into effect at a tempo beyond the imagining of any team in the world, with the possible exceptions of Australia, France and, on the most recent available evidence, Wales. Nor could he be blamed for the paucity of attacking talent available to him.

All the same, the World Cup-winning coach was culpable. If there was a logic underpinning his decision to expand the tour squad by eight or nine players, he should have pushed for an extra two or three matches – not to give each player enough rugby to make the trip worthwhile, for no one beats New Zealand on the soft-hearted basis of being all things to all men, but to ensure his combinations would reach Christchurch, the venue for the first Test, in a reasonable state of familiarity. At the very least, he should have run his putative Test side against both the Maori in Hamilton and Otago in Dunedin. By not doing so, he asked too much of the players who took the field at Jade Stadium (or Lancaster Park, as all right-thinking people continue to refer to it).

As it turned out, he picked the wrong team anyway. Robinson should not have been anywhere near the Saturday side; having arrived late because of his wife's troublesome pregnancy, he performed as though his thoughts were on other, more important things than rugby. Wilkinson found himself out of position at inside centre – an unreasonable demand, given that he barely knew what it was to play in his right position after month upon month of bodily malfunctions. Shane Byrne at hooker? One of the coaches described him, apparently with enthusiasm, as a 'busier version of Dorian West', which said all that needed saying about his shortage of class. Ben Kay at lock? Please. He had not fired a shot since the 2003 World Cup. If Leicester had been reluctant to select him for important matches, what in the name of God was Woodward thinking of, throwing him up against Chris Jack and Ali Williams? Neil Back at open-side flanker? At 36, he had played only one match since being badly undone by Joe Worsley of Wasps in the Zurich Premiership final. If ever there was a case of a game too many, this was it.

Consequences? They were severe. As the weather closed in on Christchurch in the hours leading towards kick-off – an entire winter's weather in one night, as the poor saps sitting in the open areas of the stadium discovered to their misery – the Lions' chances of making some sense of the series disappeared into the sleet-filled sky. The tourists scrummaged passably well but nowhere near aggressively enough to establish dominance, while their line out imploded as Williams stole ball after ball from the languishing Kay. Everything the All Blacks tried, they tried from the front foot. They scored only two tries, through the elongated Williams, who had the game of his life, and Sivivatu, the fastest slow-motion runner ever seen. They might as well have scored two dozen, for the Lions had nothing to throw back at them.

By way of adding insult to injury, Woodward and his 'media consultant' Alastair Campbell (wrong man, wrong place, wrong appointment) attempted to undermine the New Zealanders by going after Umaga and the Auckland hooker Keven Mealamu in respect of the now infamous 'spear tackle' on

Brian O'Driscoll, perhaps the one Lions back capable of living with the All Black attackers. O'Driscoll, his right shoulder as dislocated as could be, had been tipped into the air at a ruck 40 seconds into the game. What happened next – and there was no video evidence to shed light on the matter – was the subject of ferocious and extremely personal discussion for the next six days. Did the two All Blacks simply allow him to fall (the most charitable view)? Or did one or both of them drive him into the turf with something approaching extreme prejudice (as the Lions maintained)?

Woodward paid a midnight visit to the principal media hotel to argue his case, then rose at the crack of dawn for another go. Later on that Sunday, after the flight to Wellington, the Lions held a third public session, during which they ran through the film footage that had been considered, and dismissed, by a particularly charmless citing commissioner from South Africa. Not even the most myopic Lions follower could claim, hand on heart, that the tapes told the full story. Yes, it had been a reckless tackle; yes, both Umaga and Mealamu should have been called to account. But natural justice would have seen both of them walk free, to resume their eye-catching roles in the series. The fact that O'Driscoll was out of the tour, sickeningly and heartbreakingly, could not be held as a reason to massage the facts of the matter.

LEFT Gareth Thomas, replacement tour skipper for the injured Brian O'Driscoll, heads for the line to give the Lions a flying start to the second Test with a try after 90 seconds.

ABOVE Lions head coach Sir Clive Woodward talks the press through film footage of the incident that led to the injury to Brian O'Driscoll.

ABOVE Gordon Bulloch (right) in action against Bay of Plenty. The Scotland hooker went on to enjoy success as a midweek captain and came off the bench to win a cap in the final Test.

FACING PAGE Successful All Black captain Tana Umaga, the most influential player in the series, as depicted by caricaturist John Ireland.

Of course, the more Woodward and his allies criticised Umaga, the darker the All Blacks' mood became and the tighter they bonded together. The following weekend, they slaughtered the Lions with a performance of astonishing grandeur, led from the outside-half position by Carter, whose two-try display was nothing short of sublime. The gulf between the two sides, disconcertingly wide in Christchurch, was now a chasm of infernal dimensions. This match would have been a severe test of the Lions in mind and soul as well as body, even had relations between the two sides been amicable. Given the animosity involved, all of it generated by the tourists, the examination was too much for flesh and blood to stand.

Under the circumstances – two down with one to play – the final week was bound to be anticlimactic. The fascination, such as it was, surrounded Woodward's spirits, which had been low prior to the Wellington Test and were now positively subterranean. Contrast this with the button-bright behaviour of the second-string coaching team: Ian McGeechan, Gareth Jenkins and Mike Ford, all of whom emerged with reputations enhanced. Gordon Bulloch, the Scottish hooker, led the 'midweek massive' to a narrow but highly creditable victory over Auckland at Eden Park, where the elite side duly finished a distant second four days later. McGeechan, diplomacy made flesh, gave little away in terms of conflict between the selectors, but conflict there most definitely had been. By pushing the likes of Donncha O'Callaghan, Simon Easterby, Geordan Murphy and Mark Cueto into the senior team, McGeechan and company finally made their point.

Henry, as is his wont in victory, gave Woodward both barrels following the finale in Auckland, pointing out that the Lions' Test team had confronted All Black modernity with a game plan straight out of the Ark, ridiculing the tourists' attempts at political-style spin and adding that while the

midweek team had found their way through unbeaten, they had not played a front-line province equipped with a full hand of players. 'Had the tourists taken on the five Super 12 teams, who knows what the results would have been?' he said. Naturally, Henry knew full well how those matches would have turned out. The scorelines would not have been pretty from the Lions' perspective.

In truth, the good moments were too few by half. The Lions played pretty well in the opening 13 minutes of the very first game, Dallaglio, the conscience of the side, raising the temperature with his energetic driving play and Josh Lewsey showing a degree of brilliance that would disappear as the itinerary unfolded. Dallaglio's departure with a wrecked ankle seemed horribly significant at the time, and grew more serious by the day as the visitors were given a hurry-up by a limited Taranaki side, were soundly beaten by the Maori on an emotion-charged second Saturday and were forced to fight hard by an understrength Wellington, an out-of-form Otago and an unrated Southland team that should have been obliterated by a 70-point margin, rather than subdued by a 10-point one.

ABOVE Despite the result of the series thousands of Lions fans who made the long trip to New Zealand had a great time. Some found themselves in the stand sitting alongside an injured Lawrence Dallaglio while others **(BELOW)** caused anxious moments by indulging in the country's favourite pastime – bungy jumping.

Encouraging points? Charlie Hodgson, the form outside half in the party but never a serious contender for Test preferment, played beautifully throughout. Dwayne Peel was a force at scrum half, albeit an accident-prone one, while Matt Dawson fronted up in characteristically bold style as his aged understudy. Ryan Jones, Lewis Moody and the athletic Easterby combined well enough in the back row, Jones being the revelation of the tour with his dynamic running in the heavy traffic. That, unfortunately, was about it. Not much of a return on a £9 million investment.

New Zealand, meanwhile, were a class apart, and in Umaga, the dreadlocked dreadnought in midfield, they possessed the single most influential player on view. Theirs was an all-weather, all-purpose, all-singing, all-dancing act, compared with which the Lions were an old-fashioned side playing an old-fashioned game. The only new thing about them was the scale of the organisation. And as 15,000 visiting supporters witnessed at first hand, organisation alone is no winner, especially when the players themselves are overstretched, overmatched and, in some cases, over the hill.

INTERNATIONAL SCENE

And Then There Were 14
the Super 12 Expands

by RAECHELLE EDWARDS

"'There will be plenty of tough times for us over the next year, and every year, so it's a matter of persevering with what we believe in and sticking to our guiding principles ...'"

After ten very successful years the southern hemisphere's premier provincial rugby competition, Super 12, is set for a growth phase with the addition of two new teams and 26 extra matches. Adding these new teams is all about product – increasing match time for the pay TV providers in Australia, New Zealand, South Africa and the United Kingdom, who rely heavily on quality sports coverage to drive revenue.

RIGHT Former All Black No. 8 and coach John Mitchell is the man in charge at Western Force.

FACING PAGE Rugby WA chairman Geoff Stooke (left) and Western Force chief executive officer Peter O'Meara at the April 2005 presentation in Perth that introduced the new name and logo to the rugby world.

After a highly competitive tendering process, the two new teams to play in the 2006 Super 14 are the 'Western Force', a fourth Australian team based in Perth, and the 'Central Cheetahs', a fifth South African regional team that incorporates the Free State, Griquas and Griffons.

Almost immediately after Perth won the bid to host Australia's new team, a professional outfit emerged. The administration took shape, players began to be thoughtfully targeted and signed and an experienced and highly regarded coach was named in John Mitchell.

As a player, Mitchell was a tough No. 8 with Waikato province in New Zealand and toured England and Scotland with the All Blacks in 1993, captaining the side in three midweek matches. On his retirement, his coaching career quickly took off. He coached English club Sale, and in 1997 became assistant coach (to Clive Woodward) of the England team, a position he held for three years.

On returning to New Zealand in 2001, Mitchell was named head coach of the Waikato Chiefs in the Super 12. The next year, he replaced Wayne Smith as coach of the All Blacks, an appointment that concluded following the 2003 World Cup and a disappointing semi-final loss to Australia. He is one of three New Zealanders to have played for, captained and coached the All Blacks.

Having returned to Waikato as coach of the National Provincial Championship side, 'Mitch' moved to Perth in 2005 to take charge of the Western Force. Politically his appointment was seen by many as a sensitive decision – a Kiwi coaching an Australian provincial side for the first time. 'Western Australia went down the road that they wanted to pick the best coach available and he was definitely the best coach available,' says Wallaby coach Eddie Jones.

Mitchell says, 'Clearly I'm very grateful and fortunate to be head coach in one of the toughest competitions in the world and somebody has had the foresight to understand that I can actually add value to Australian rugby.

NEXT

ARE PROUD TO SUPPORT

WOODEN SPOON RUGBY WORLD '06

'I've always secretly admired Australians' attitude in their positive outlook on life and I guess I have a very similar outlook on life so it's something that doesn't really worry me coming to Australia.'

Mitchell's coaching style has evolved 'from being a fitness director to a more player specific coach. I seek a lot of my solutions and get advice through questioning, more than just telling players what to do.

'Being an inaugural head coach uniting with everyone else as a foundation member we can all get together and put on the table examples of best practice and examples of poor practice,' he says. 'We can create an environment we want to be a part of ... it's easier to start a culture than to change an inherited one and that excites me.'

Being unencumbered by tradition gives the Western Force a rare opportunity to create something special. Wallaby Nathan Sharpe says, 'The biggest factor in making the decision to sign [with the Western Force] was that in a professional rugby career it's a once-off opportunity to be involved in something where you're starting a team from scratch in a city that I've been to quite a few times and I really like, so it's just an opportunity that's too good to knock back.

BELOW Western Force signing Nathan Sharpe, formerly of Queensland, nabs line-out ball for the Wallabies against Italy at Melbourne in June 2005.

'There's no set ways of doing things when you come into that organisation, there's no preconceptions about the way things are done and that's something that is rare in any organisation.'

Sharpe and Mitchell both have high, but realistic, expectations for their new side. Says Mitchell, 'You only have to look at successful contact sports teams in the southern hemisphere that are now recognised as very good programs, such as the West Coast Eagles – they took five to six years; so did the Broncos and the Brumbies.

'There will be plenty of tough times for us over the next year, and every year, so it's a matter of persevering with what we believe in and sticking to our guiding principles and we'll eventually get there.'

Sharpe agrees. 'Were looking for a successful season and by that I mean winning more than we lose and if we can do that then I think we'll be very happy.

'You look at teams like the Canterbury Crusaders and you look at the success of their teams – it's all based on their culture; they've got that winning way and that keeps resurfacing each year.'

The Western Force have signed three high-profile players in Sharpe, Brendan Cannon and Matt Henjak, whose role as leaders will naturally influence and direct the team.

Mitchell talks about his recruitment process. 'With players we identified the core leaders we would like to attract here, and they are the players we would really like to cement the culture and live and act the standards we set. They are critical and they will help younger players find their feet.'

The Western Force have also signed former Wallaby John Welborn, who grew up in Perth. Welborn has recently been playing in France. 'He'll not only be competitive in fighting for a spot in the XV but he'll also be able to pass on a lot of fantastic knowledge to younger players, and we're currently in the process of preparing our academy and ... a lot of our locals will come up through that system,' said Mitchell.

Eddie Jones hopes this new team will start to have a positive impact quickly on Australian rugby, since the talent pool he has to choose from will increase by 25 per cent.

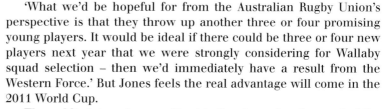

'What we'd be hopeful for from the Australian Rugby Union's perspective is that they throw up another three or four promising young players. It would be ideal if there could be three or four new players next year that we were strongly considering for Wallaby squad selection – then we'd immediately have a result from the Western Force.' But Jones feels the real advantage will come in the 2011 World Cup.

The public interest was evident in the strong involvement of the Perth community in the nine-month process to decide the name of the team, even though it's not a traditional rugby city. The administration is putting plans into place to support the growth of the game in Western Australia. Mitchell is ambitious, wanting the Force to become the 'best program in the southern hemisphere' in time. He is committed to creating the foundations that lead to long-term success.

The selection process and set-up for the Central Cheetahs has not been as smooth in a very political South African rugby environment. In contrast to the Western Force's professional attitude and the Australian Rugby Union's policy to back the new side and give them the latitude to develop and grow a culture of success, the Central Cheetahs have been named as South Africa's fifth side in the 2006 Super 14 competition but they are not guaranteed to remain in 2007.

The lowest-placed South African side at the completion of the 2006 Super 14 tournament will be replaced by the South Eastern Cape franchise. At the end of the 2007 Super 14 season, the South African franchise team that is last on the Super 14 log, excluding the South Eastern Cape, will play in a promotion-relegation match against the franchise team that did not play in the 2007 Super 14 competition. South African Rugby has promised the South Eastern Cape financial assistance to help prepare for the Super 14 in 2007 and 2008.

'I think we have a fair system, because if you get the results, you stay and if you do not perform, you are away,' says South African Rugby president Brian van Rooyen. Whether the system is fair or not

LEFT Time to call it a day. Rassie Erasmus takes a heavy hit from Kees Lensing of the Blue Bulls as the Free State Cheetahs go down in the final of the 2004 Currie Cup. This was Erasmus's last match as a player before retirement. He went on to coach the Free State outfit and now has the top job with the Central Cheetahs Super 14 side.

is questionable. What is clear is the pressure this decision places on the Cheetahs to perform in their inaugural Super 14 season.

Wallaby coach Jones says that South Africa easily has the talent to put a fifth side on the park, especially considering the number of players who have followed offers overseas. 'The only question is how successfully they can administer it. I think it's been shown that the sides that are well administered and well coached will do well.'

Former Springbok Johan 'Rassie' Erasmus has been appointed coach of the Cheetahs; of the administration he says, 'All I can tell you is that it will be handled by all three unions [Free State, Griquas and Griffons] in the various departments.'

Erasmus retired from rugby at the end of 2004, having captained the Cheetahs in their defeat to the Blue Bulls in the Currie Cup. He feels that honesty and teamwork will be the critical factors in the success of the team because it involves the merging of three provinces.

'I know the quality of players we produce in the region and I know if we can keep them here we will definitely be very competitive.'

The Cheetahs have signed current and former Springboks Os du Randt, Naka Drotske, CJ van der Linde, Ollie le Roux and Michael Claassen, as well as South African sevens players Eddie Fredericks, Anton Pitout and Dale Heidtmann.

BELOW Cheetahs signing Os du Randt (right) with John Smit and Ernie Els after the golfer had presented the Springboks with their jerseys ahead of the November 2004 clash with England at Twickenham.

Erasmus sees the main challenge for the team based in Bloemfontein as 'making it a winning team, while being representative of all the three unions, so that we can get a good support base. Like all other coaches I will be judged if my team is winning or not.'

The Cheetahs are hoping to be competitive and avoid relegation at the end of the 2006 Super 14 competition, so they have the opportunity to continue their development. But achieving this success will be tough, as they won't be creating a new culture; they'll be attempting to pull together the interests of three different provinces, each with its own agenda, while desperately chasing short-term success.

International Sevens
an Epic Season Marred

by NIGEL STARMER-SMITH

'I had a sense of foreboding ... when a member of the Executive Board of the IOC ... remarked that he regarded rugby sevens "as something of a joke".'

ABOVE Fiji sevens sensation William Ryder tries to evade the All Black cover in the final of the 2005 Rugby World Cup Sevens in Hong Kong.

Amidst the euphoria that greeted the selection of London as the host city for the 2012 Olympic Games, something was lost; something that bitterly disappointed me and many millions around the world who know and love the global game of rugby sevens. The day following that announcement the International Olympic Committee, having discarded softball and baseball from their schedule of Olympic sports, voted not to include sevens as a new sport in the schedule. It was a crass decision, which almost defies belief, provoking a response of anger, frustration and incredulity on every continent. Rugby sevens didn't even make the 'play-off' vote between the five potential 'replacement' sports, as the final choice concerned just karate and squash – though in the end neither of those received sufficient support to win inclusion.

I had a sense of foreboding about the whole sad saga from the moment the month before when a member of the Executive Board of the IOC, American Dennis Oswald, clearly an influential figure in these deliberations, remarked that he regarded rugby sevens 'as something of a joke'. I am given to understand that the man has never attended a rugby sevens event. How well qualified does that make him to express such an absurd, yet destructive, observation and then to have a vital part in the making of such an important decision? I was in Paris at the time that his remark was made public, attending the IRB Sevens tournament there, and the response from the 16 participating nations was one of sheer disbelief and absolute fury at such an insult. The captains of all the competing teams immediately sent a letter of protest to the IOC president, expressing their complete disgust.

BELOW Clark Laidlaw takes on Australia as Scotland go down to the Wallabies in the final of the Plate competition at the Wellington Sevens in February.

Seven-a-side rugby fulfils all the criteria for inclusion as an Olympic sport. Its origins go back as far as 1883, to Ned Haig and Melrose in Scotland, and it has grown dramatically in the past 30 years to the extent that there can be few sports – football may be the only one, in fact – played in as many countries. Eighty nations, spanning every

continent, entered this year's Rugby World Cup Sevens (the first was in 1993) and competed in 14 qualifying tournaments around the world. Twenty-four nations took part in the finals – with representation from Tunisia to Tonga, Chinese Taipei to Canada, Korea to Kenya, the USA to Uruguay. A capacity crowd of 40,000 witnessed the event over three days; it was won by Fiji, a nation which I doubt has any prospect whatsoever of making a final, let alone of winning a medal, in any existing Olympic sport.

For the past six seasons more than 40 countries have participated in the annual IRB Sevens Series, taking the game each year to up to ten different venues spanning every continent. The spectacle is thrilling; the skill levels exceptional; the format well established and fair; the discipline – and player self-discipline – equal to that in any sport; the competition intense; and the results unpredictable. Tournament title winners have come from South America, Africa, Europe, Australasia and Oceania within one season. I have seen Kenya beat Australia, Tunisia beat South Africa, Samoa beat New Zealand, Georgia beat England, and so on. It is that capacity for all to be competitive that not only generates such wonderful spectator enthusiasm and excitement but has encouraged such a dramatic growth in the worldwide popularity of the sport amongst nations who know they cannot compete meaningfully on the world stage in so many other games.

Perhaps we have become too patronising and complacent as we applaud the Olympic swimmer from Niue who is lapped twice in the Olympic pool, or the Uruguayan team that finishes half a lap behind in the track relay event. Taking part is one thing, having a real chance of some success is another – and one of the beauties of sevens is that there is no such thing as a 'no-hoper'. What is even more important, surely, is that rugby in the form of seven-a-side offers to so many nations, and so many sportsmen – and indeed sportswomen, who are likewise taking up the sport in great numbers – the goal of actually qualifying for an Olympics, when so many current Olympic sports have such limited interest or participation on the world stage: rowing, wrestling, handball, cycling, synchronised swimming and so on. And if anyone should doubt the true appeal of sevens on a global scale, for the watcher as well as the participant, then consider the fact that there has been, by common consent, no more successful team sport at the recent Commonwealth Games, Asian Games and World Games than rugby sevens.

In terms of the expansion of world sport, the exclusion of sevens from the Olympic Games is verging on scandalous; it represents an enormous loss of opportunity by a movement that claimed it wanted to move with the times. The boost to the development of the game through the consequential added financial and human resources and support that its inclusion in the Olympic programme would have provided can only be guessed at. But I know that a two-day spectacular event at Twickenham or the new Olympic Stadium in 2012 would have been for sure one of the memorable highlights of the London Olympiad – and in all probability would have been the sport for which tickets would have sold out first. Perhaps one day somebody who knows will explain to me and all those involved in this worldwide sport why rugby sevens was cast aside. There are many thousands of youngsters, learning the arts of their national sport, running barefoot on the scruffy, unmarked, sunbaked patches of wasteland that pass as rugby pitches in the South Sea islands, and by contrast many other young men and women running with a rugby ball in hand, defying the cold on snow-covered open spaces this winter on the European Steppes of the former satellite states of the USSR – all of whom want, and deserve, an answer.

If subsequent events have cast something of a shadow over the sevens season, nothing will diminish the memory of a spectacular Rugby World Cup Sevens in Hong Kong last March. Twenty-four nations took part in the finals, from an original figure of eighty who entered the qualifying tournaments or qualified direct as one of the top eight seeds together with host union Hong Kong. From start to finish it was a magnificent three-day event, and if anyone has any lingering doubts about the spectacular skills and quality of seven-a-side rugby, its status as a global team sport or its power to captivate and enthral, then they must have missed this fourth World Cup in its entirety. Juan Martin Stefani accompanied the Uruguayan squad as team doctor to this their first-ever World Cup finals and he summed up the experience in these words: 'It was amazing; I was one of the lucky fans to have lived this unbelievable event from the inside … with its own very special aura provided by the players, and an incredible crowd.' After 81 games between the teams – playing 'round robin' in four pools of six teams on the first two days, followed by all the knockout rounds for the four

LEFT Fiji's Waisale Serevi consoles Ben Gollings after the South Sea islanders had put England out of the RWC Sevens competition in a tense semi-final.

FACING PAGE The All Blacks did not win the World Cup but they did retain their IRB Sevens title for the sixth consecutive year. Here they celebrate after victory in the Wellington Sevens.

different trophy levels on day three – the outcome was a fairy-tale finale for Fiji, who had not won a major international tournament since the IRB Sevens in George, South Africa, in 2002.

The tone of unrelenting excitement was established from the moment – 9.43 a.m. on day one, in the fifth tie of the tournament – that Tunisia and South Africa took the field. Tunisia, a country where sevens has taken a strong hold, overcame the number five seeds 19-12. From that moment nobody felt secure. Even New Zealand, reigning world champions and winners of their last three IRB Sevens tournaments prior to Hong Kong, were given a mighty scare by Tonga and won in the end by the margin of just one converted try. Against the odds Italy drew with Georgia, whilst, typically, France, with a Gallic shrug, upset England, the second-favourites and reigning three-time Hong Kong winners, 28-17.

But eventually the cream came to the top and the final day was captivating from first to last. The later knockout rounds provided a sequence of sevens that could scarce be surpassed for quality of play or excitement. Australia, a young squad based on the U21 Wallabies, beat South Africa 15-14 at the Cup quarter-final stage, whilst Fiji overcame Argentina 22-14 in a clash of experience, mercurial touches, pace and power versus an indefatigable Pumas side with an amazing defence. They joined England and New Zealand in the semi-finals for two games which should be required viewing for any aspiring sevens player. New Zealand, inspired by a rejuvenated Amasio Valence and supremely led by young Liam Messam, clung on to win with six players as Australia failed to exploit a crucial overlap in the dying seconds; 24-20 the final score. In the second semi-final, Fiji versus England, a 'sudden-death' try was required to separate two teams who provided another wondrous display. England scored an equalising try in the last second of normal time, and the brilliant Ben Gollings missed what would have been the winning conversion from wide out by no more than a few inches. But it was as if the outcome had been pre-ordained; and no doubt many prayers were being offered up back home in the South Sea island nation by people riveted to the live TV coverage, as the 'Maestro', sevens legend Waisale Serevi, just one month short of his 37th birthday, shot away on the blind side, more these days a case of deft footwork and guile than explosive pace, to reach the far corner for the winning try.

Nor was the final of any lower quality, as one wondered whether the returning former stars of Fijian rugby, garnered from around the world for this event by national coach Wayne Pivac and

Serevi himself, and after just two weeks' preparation together, could turn it on just one more time against the pace, strength and established teamwork of Gordon Tietjens' New Zealand squad. But the power and ground-eating pace, and those characteristic mercurial handling skills, had not deserted the likes of Isireli Bobo, Jone Daunivucu, man-mountain Semisi Naevo, the Satala brothers, Vilimoni Delasau and the outstanding newcomers this season – William Ryder and Neumi Nanuku – plus of course, Serevi. It was a magnificent contest – try for try, tackle for tackle – and a long time before Fiji could gain the upper hand over a New Zealand team that had been cruelly deprived through injury of the brilliant Orene Ai'i and Tafai Ioasa. Only at the very end did the brave men in black wilt under the sustained power and pace of the irresistible Fijians. A fabulous end to an unforgettable experience for those lucky enough to have been in the Hong Kong Stadium.

I wouldn't be surprised if the celebrations are still going on. Ten thousand turned up at Nadi Airport to greet their returning heroes, preceding a parade across the island that took the best part of a day before a further 40,000 thronged the National Stadium to welcome and salute the Fijian team. The prime minister declared a national holiday in celebration. And so for the second time Waisale Serevi, Player of the Tournament (how could my two fellow judges and I choose anyone else?), had guided Fiji to the IRB World Sevens crown, the Melrose Cup. The trophy was back in the hands of those who cherish it the most.

There was to be some real consolation for New Zealand, who had failed so narrowly to take the trophy they most desired, for they once again, for the sixth year out of six, retained the title of overall IRB Sevens champions. It was an extraordinary achievement, notably by their retiring (after the Commonwealth Games) coach and mentor, Gordon Tietjens, who has had charge of New Zealand sevens since 1994. He has set the standard for sevens rugby for the world. His squad has won every title on offer along the way – IRB Sevens, Commonwealth and World crowns. This season New Zealand won the IRB tournaments in South Africa, New Zealand, the USA and Singapore – whilst England won in Dubai; South Africa in London; and, for their first-ever title, France in Paris. Gordon Tietjens will leave a remarkable legacy, and I salute him for all that he has achieved, not only for New Zealand but more importantly for the game of sevens itself.

The Next in Line
the U19 and U21 World Championships

by **ALAN LORIMER**

'In the event the first three positions were predictably occupied by the Big Three from the southern hemisphere. Home Union U21 rugby still lags some distance behind.'

The year 2005 was, without doubt, as good a vintage for South Africa as a Boschendal best, after the country's young players celebrated a double success with global titles at U19 and U21 age levels. It was exactly what South African rugby needed at a time when the national game is going through a turbulent period. It was a clear message, too, that multiracial rugby in South Africa is working. This was the future of Springbok rugby.

Durban, hosting the U19 tournament in March/April for a second successive year, provided the platform for South Africa to achieve the first part of their mission. The junior Boks defeated the title

holders, New Zealand, in a tense final that demonstrated the young South Africans' all-round game and notably the pace of their back three. There will be undoubtedly a number of stars to emerge from this Baby Bok side, but already the name of outside half Jody Rose must be high on the potential contracts list. Others to show up well for South Africa were No. 8 Pieter Myburgh, hooker Mahlatse Ralepelle, back-rower Hilton Lobberts, and full back Shandre Frolick.

> **ABOVE** South Africa U19 back-row forward Hilton Lobberts offloads in the tackle during the hosts' 15-9 victory over France.
>
> **FACING PAGE** South Africa celebrate becoming IRB U19 world champions.

The consensus at the championship was that this was not such a star-studded New Zealand side as that which won in 2004. Nevertheless there were players who will surely figure at higher levels, among them centre Isaia Toeava, who has already played in the IRB World Sevens Series, fellow centre Tim Bateman and fiery flankers George Whitelock and Vern Kamo.

If New Zealand were less strong this year then the opposite was true of Australia, who made an immediate impact on the championship with a 10-6 win over France in the opener. Outstanding for Australia and a player surely destined to be a full Wallaby was outside half Mathew Brandon. You had for once to feel sympathy for the Aussies, who just missed out on a place in the final after losing in the penultimate round to New Zealand in a penalty shoot-out, after the teams had finished level, 25-25, at full time.

Of the Six Nations countries, it was England who provided the strongest challenge, their fourth-place finish confirming an academy system now functioning efficiently. England's production line will benefit from a good showing by the U19s, among whom loose-head prop Dylan Hartley, No. 8 Jordan Crane and Gloucester centre Anthony Allen all look good prospects.

In the case of Wales, who played some exhilarating rugby in the mould of their senior team to stack up a table-topping 21 tries in the pool stages, look out for advancement from centres Tom

FACING PAGE New Zealand's Hosea Gear, brother of All Black Rico and a Super 12 player with the Hurricanes, on the attack during his side's 60-15 victory over Wales U21.

BELOW Australia and Argentina contest a line out as the Wallaby U21 side defeat the hosts 25-20.

Cheeseman and Jonathan Spratt, tight-head prop Craig Mitchell and athletic lock Will Jones.

Wales lost to France in the fifth-place play-off thanks to a last-minute dropped goal, but overall they should be pleased with a good performance in the championship. Not so France, who despite a rigorous and lengthy preparation for the tournament slipped from second to fifth. Perhaps lacking the quality players of last season, France still had some exciting performers, the pick of them being flanker Marc Giraud and full back Maxime Médard, the latter already having played in the Heineken Cup for Toulouse.

Elsewhere, ninth-place finishers Ireland, with undoubtedly the toughest of draws, have potential stars in full back Rob Kearney, centres Fergus McFadden and Darren Cave, No. 8 Diarmuid Laffen and flanker Barry O'Mahony, while Celtic cousins Scotland can look to the future with players like flanker Ross Rennie and prop Kyle Traynor capable of making the next step.

There seemed to be only a brief pause post-Durban before the U21s occupied centre stage in the attractive Argentinian city of Mendoza, whose dry winter weather and upgraded club facilities made it a popular choice for the competition. World rugby had come to Mendoza, and the city responded by embracing its sporting guests with a warmth and enthusiasm that helped make the 2005 championship a memorable event.

From the outset it was clear that the southern hemisphere countries, with the advantage of playing in season and with players already competitively honed by Super 12 rugby, would dominate the tournament. In the event the first three positions were predictably occupied by the Big Three from the southern hemisphere. Home Union U21 rugby still lags some distance behind.

It was South Africa against Australia in the final in front of a 28,000 crowd at the 1978 soccer World Cup venue Estadio Malvinas Argentinas. The young Boks appeared to have the game under control, only for Australia's late challenge to produce a scoreline of 24-20. South Africa were the winners, but Australia showed that they are raising their game at this level. Only France provided the northern hemisphere cheerleaders with anything to shout about, but in the third-place play-off there was only one team in the running. New Zealand, disappointed at losing to South Africa in the penultimate round, vented their frustration on the French to win 47-21.

And the stars from the top four? From South Africa expect to hear more of hooker Chiliboy

Ralepelle, outside half Morne Steyn (already a Super 12 player), No. 8 Pieter Louw, centres Thabang Molefe and Earl Rose, and full back Hendrik Daniller. Watch, too, for further progress among Australians from hooker Tatafu Polota-Nau, wing Digby Ioane, and full back Cameron Shepherd. And ready to join the ranks of New Zealand's seemingly overstocked larder of senior talent are scrum half Andrew Ellis, wing Hosea Gear and flanker Liam Messam.

France, who blew *chaud et froid* in the tournament, had exciting players in Maxime Médard, promoted from the U19s and operating on the wing, full back Jean-Baptiste Peyras and centre Sylvain Mirande. For hosts Argentina, who finished on a high note with a 39-7 win over Scotland in the fifth-place play-off, there was evidence of quality play from Matias Cortese at hooker, Jose Guzman at No. 8 and Joaquin Brinnand at full back; there was also confirmation that their three capped players, Gonzalo Tiesi, Manuel Carizza and Agustin Creevy, are worthy of this honour.

Top among the Home Unions, and providing something of a boost for the game north of the border after two poor seasons at senior level, were Scotland. Coached by former Test No. 8 Iain Paxton, Scotland did well to take a bonus point from their opening match against Australia and looked the part when defeating Wales in round four. With the senior ranks in Scotland scarcely awash with talent, there are genuine opportunities for the young Scots, among whom No. 8 John Beattie, scrum half Alasdhair McFarlane and tight-head prop Moray Low excelled.

England, who had good displays from lock Richard Blaze, occupied seventh place after defeating an out-of-sorts and depleted Wales side in a high-scoring match. But Wales may reflect that what is essentially a development exercise confirmed the talent of outside half Aled Thomas, centre Andrew Bishop and prop Cai Griffiths. Meanwhile, Ireland, runners-up last year and with three victories from five rounds, were much better than their ninth-place finish suggests. They can look to the likes of prodigious goal-kicker Gareth Steenson (the Dungannon outside half) and No. 8 Stephen Ferris putting pressure on more established players.

Elsewhere, Samoa fully justified their inclusion in the 2005 tournament, while Canada – every team's whipping boys until the final round when they pulled off a surprise 33-30 win over Italy – showed that with better preparation coming into the championship they could live with the stronger sides. Which left Italy at the bottom of the pile and theoretically out of the 2006 championship. That will be held in France and might just offer the host nation the opportunity to show that they too can produce more than vintage wines.

Many languages, one meaning

☑ **W**e do our best to make sure Cathay Pacific means welcome in any language, wherever in the world you are travelling with us. All our flight attendants are bilingual and they will do everything they can to make you feel at home. It's the little things we remember.

Now you're really flying.

Voted Airline of the Year 2005 in Skytrax passenger survey.

www.cathaypacific.com

CATHAY PACIFIC

Airline of the Year 2005

Canada Clean Up
the 2005 IRB Super Cup

by CHRIS THAU

'The hard work of the industrious Canadians was rewarded with tries by rookies Brodie Henderson and Dean Van Camp, both of whom were making their debuts in Canadian colours.'

The IRB Super Cup concept is not new. Originally it was launched, in a different context and format, as the IRB Superpowers Cup – the brainchild of the late Vernon Pugh, the innovative IRB chairman who sadly died two years ago. Pugh understood early on that the current structure of the international game, dominated by the eight foundation unions, the original members of the IRFB (England, Scotland, Ireland, Wales, France, South Africa, New Zealand and Australia), is unhealthy and detrimental to the global development of rugby. He advocated the implementation of a structured programme aimed at doubling the number of elite teams.

The IRB planners argued that, with Argentina and Italy already knocking at the door of the elite, by increasing the quantity and quality of the tuition, preparation and financial support for the countries described as the Tier Two nations (Romania, Fiji, Samoa, Tonga, Canada, the USA and Japan) their playing standard and competitive edge would go up. In turn this would increase the credibility and drawing power of RWC, the jewel in the game's crown and the main revenue provider for world rugby.

The Superpowers Cup was a project aimed at giving Tier Two nations an opportunity to consistently compete among themselves to increase their playing standards, and also at giving China an opportunity to test themselves against the big boys. The original tournament, scheduled for 2003 and to involve the USA, Russia, Japan and China, was cut back to three competitors when China did not take part due to the outbreak of the SARS epidemic in Asia. From a rugby point of view, the absence of the Chinese may have been a blessing in disguise, as their playing standard was well below that of the other three countries and the likely mismatches would have acted as a disincentive for the young Chinese Federation.

The following year, the tournament, renamed the IRB Super Cup and sponsored by Toshiba, was held in Tokyo, with Canada replacing the Chinese. This produced very spectacular and, with the exception of the Russian games, competitive matches. Japan beat Canada in the final to win the tournament, and a subsequent competition was pencilled in, with Romania replacing Russia, as the IRB launched its strategic plan designed to speed up the development of Tier Two countries.

So, the 2nd IRB Super Cup, once again sponsored by Toshiba, kicked off on 24 May 2005 at Tokyo's Prince Chichibu Stadium, the home of Japan RFU, with the match between the USA and Canada. Both US coach Tom Billups and his Canadian counterpart, Ric Suggitt, described the event as a godsend as the two North American teams prepared for battle. The two were also delighted with the opportunity provided by the event to build up for the Test matches against Wales and for the Churchill Cup, all which took place soon afterwards.

LEFT Japan's new head coach, Jean-Pierre Elissalde, father of France international scrum half Jean-Baptiste.

FACING PAGE Canada and the USA Eagles battle it out at the Prince Chichibu Stadium, Tokyo.

PREVIOUS PAGE Veteran Canadian prop Kevin Tkachuk, who came off the bench late in the first half of the final, runs into Takashi Tsuji and Hirotoki Onozawa.

'This is a great opportunity for our young players to establish themselves within a very competitive environment, for which we thank both the IRB and the Japan Union. We have not been able to bring our best team, as many of our top players who play for French clubs have been unable to travel. This will definitely hamper our potential, but on the other hand it will help the younger players make an impact at international level,' Romanian technical director Robert Antonin said.

Japan's priorities were fairly similar. 'For us the first match is an opportunity to revenge our narrow defeat by Romania last autumn in Bucharest, and regain credibility with the Japanese fans,' Japan coach and former international scrum half Mitsutake Hagimoto said.

'Overall, the tournament offers a unique opportunity to experiment and further develop our new playing style, with the help of French coaches Jean-Pierre Elissalde and Edmond Jourda. This is a valuable initiative which helps us a lot,' Hagimoto added.

'The fact that it is impossible to say who will win the tournament gives a clear indication of the quality of the field and of how closely matched the four teams are – the ingredients of a week of top-quality rugby in Tokyo,' IRB tournament director Mark Egan said.

Canada featured five newcomers in the starting line-up, including Luke Tait of Wales U19 and U21 fame, David Ramsay at lock forward and Aaron Carpenter at No. 8. They twice came from behind to narrowly defeat their neighbours and rivals 30-26. In the second match Japan defeated a vigorous but somewhat naive Romania 23-16 to secure a repeat of last year's final.

The Romanians took an early lead through a try by captain Gabriel Brezoianu, playing at centre in the absence of incumbents Romeo Gontineac and Valentin Maftei, who were unable to travel to Japan due to club commitments in France. The Romanian forwards, also deprived of several first-choice players (Balan, Tonita, Petrichei, etc), controlled the game with authority, but failed to convert the pressure into points, which cost them dearly in a tense and emotional finale. In the event, Daisuke Ohata, who had scored some ten minutes into the second half after an intense period of Japanese pressure, stole the limelight with a second, late try that broke the 16-all stalemate and with it Romanian hearts.

In the play-off for the bronze medal, the superior size and strength of the USA pack tilted the balance in the Americans' favour. Although the Romanians had the last word with a try by lock

ABOVE Debutant wing Brodie Henderson crosses for Canada's first try of the final.

FACING PAGE Centre Dean Van Camp, also playing in his first international, runs in Canada's second try.

forward George Oprisor in injury time, it was too little too late. The USA Eagles had already sealed the match, which ended 28-22, with tries by David Fee and Mike Paleafu, craftily orchestrated by fly half Mike Hercus. 'It was a sound performance and we take heart from the quality displayed by the team,' captain Kort Schubert said.

In the final, it was the turn of Canada to show composure and adaptability as they turned the tables on their hosts, after a match of great intensity, to claim the trophy. They fought manfully to win 15-10 after a first half in which the two sides tackled each other to a standstill. It was Canadian coach Suggitt's decision to replace his two props just before half-time that changed the shape of the game, and the Canadian fortunes, as the two veterans Kevin Tkachuk and Garth Cooke added edge to the team effort.

The hard work of the industrious Canadians was rewarded with tries by rookies Brodie Henderson and Dean Van Camp, both of whom were making their debuts in Canadian colours. 'The

boys applied themselves and deserved this win thoroughly. It takes a while to get used to winning silverware but it was a long way coming. I am very happy for the team,' Suggitt observed.

'From the IRB's point of view, this tournament plays a very important role in respect to the strategic initiatives we wish to develop around the IRB Tier Two unions programme,' the IRB's Mark Egan said after the event.

'The very tight scorelines tell volumes about the very close encounters and how valuable these clashes have been for the participants. We are currently reviewing the IRB Tier Two programme with the view of meeting one of our key strategic goals, which is to increase the number and competitiveness of the unions at Tier One level,' he added.

The tournament enabled the IRB high performance consultant, Daniel Collins of Australia, to evaluate the diverse requirements of the four unions, while providing a good benchmark for the work that needs to be done. The IRB Council has committed substantial amounts to this four-year project, and the first structure is about to materialise with the launch of a Pan-Pacific tournament, involving Japan, Samoa, Fiji and Tonga plus the four Australian Super 14 franchises.

The Road to France
RWC 2007 Round-up

by CHRIS THAU

'With their scrum in dominant mood, China snatched victory from the jaws of defeat in the last minutes of play. The score stood at 17-19 as their huge second row Ma Bing crashed over ...'

By the end of 2005, nearly two-thirds of the gigantic qualifying programme for the sixth RWC will have been completed. Involving 87 of the IRB's unions, the four-year cycle of RWC 2007 commenced in September 2004, in Andorra la Vella, the capital of the Principality of Andorra. The hosts, Andorra, coached by former New Zealand Maori hooker Bruce Hemara, demolished their opponents from Norway to win by 76 points to 3, with Andorra's Georgian-born hooker Josef Txelidtze scoring the first try of RWC 2007.

Two weeks later, Andorra completed the double over Norway with a 23-9 win in Bergen, the second encounter of the 194-match RWC 2007 saga. The plucky Andorrans have had the longest run in their RWC history, having passed through rounds one and two to reach round three of the European zone against the might of Spain, the Netherlands and Poland; not bad for a union boasting only about 70 players. The playing programme of the RWC starts earlier in Europe than in the other zones, due to the sheer numbers involved. By the end of 2005, the 30-odd European unions taking part will have played more than 50 of their 86 qualifying matches.

At the beginning of their RWC campaign, in round two of the European zone, Poland – once one of the powerhouses of Central and East European rugby – managed to overcome a spirited challenge to scrape home 20-15 against an abrasive and dynamic Switzerland in the Baltic port of Gdynia. The Poles finished top of their round two pool and recommence their RWC campaign against Andorra at the end of October and will finish against the Netherlands next April.

Meanwhile Malta, one of the youngest European unions, who only commenced their international adventure in the qualifying rounds of RWC 1999, surprised the world and themselves with an unexpected 17-8 away win over the Swiss, which secured them a place in the play-offs for round three. The Maltese, who had given Poland some food for thought in their round two match in Valletta (the Poles won 38-13 after a dramatic encounter), duly reached round three by beating Denmark and will kick off against the powerful Germany, so far unbeaten in the competition.

Moldova, who had beaten Denmark 20-11 in Copenhagen in round two, were unable to defeat a powerful and well-drilled Germany later in the round. The Germans won a tough match in Chisinau (Kishinev) 27-18 to make sure they finished top of the pool. If they can go on to win

RIGHT The Andorra team celebrate after their 76-3 home victory in the first leg of their round one tie against Norway. They followed up by winning the second leg 23-9.

their round three group as well, which includes the likes of Belgium, Croatia and Serbia & Montenegro, they will progress to the home-and-away knockout play-off against the top side in the other European round three pool, which includes Spain and the Netherlands.

In the Americas, divided as it is into the North (NAWIRA) and South (CONSUR), it was Brazil, in the latter zone, who got the ball rolling, commencing their qualifying campaign in October 2004 with a 73-3 victory over Peru in front of their own public in Sao Paulo. Meanwhile Venezuela, the other leading contenders, opened their campaign with a hard-fought 32-22 away victory over Peru, followed a week later by a cliffhanger in Bogota, where they managed to beat the hosts, Colombia, 31-27. A laboured 11-5 win over Venezuela in the final match secured Brazil a place in round two against the might of Chile and Paraguay. 'Although we did not play well we won and this was what counted. We have a young squad and I think we will be able to play better rugby in the next round,' Brazilian captain Alexandre Mobrige said.

Meanwhile, the NAWIRA countries commenced their RWC race with the historic encounter between their smallest unions, St Lucia and St Vincent & Grenadines, both making their RWC

debuts. St Lucia won 36-25 to qualify for the tournament to be held in Georgetown, Guyana, in August 2005. The winner in Guyana takes on Bahamas for a place in round three. The latter were the unexpected victors of the second pool, also comprising Bermuda, Cayman Islands and Jamaica. Although defeated 5-3 by Jamaica in the final group match, Bahamas managed to qualify on the strength of their earlier wins, 23-12 over Cayman Islands and 24-15 over Bermuda, combined with Jamaica's 8-18 defeat at the hands of Cayman Islands.

The first to enter the fray in Asia were the People's Republic of China. Unable to play their first match against the Arabian Gulf, due to visa problems, they put the disappointment behind them with a fine 22-19 win over their Chinese Taipei neighbours. With their scrum in dominant mood, China snatched victory from the jaws of defeat in the last minutes of play. The score stood at 17-19 as their huge second row Ma Bing crashed over to turn a two-point deficit into a three-point advantage. It was mainland China's first-ever win over Chinese Taipei, and the enthusiastic Chinese players celebrated the unexpected win long after the match ended.

Next up, the Arabian Gulf managed a valuable 30-26 win, also over Chinese Taipei. Meanwhile, Sri Lanka, making history under the astute management of George Simpkin (coaching his fourth national team after Fiji, Hong Kong and China), surprised hosts Thailand with the vigour and subtlety of their game, winning 48-38 in a match of remarkable quality. India recorded their first RWC win on home soil when they beat Malaysia 48-12 in Mumbai, although their 36-22 defeat at the hands of Kazakhstan had already put an end to their aspirations. Guam, making their RWC debut, managed an inspiring 8-8 draw against the visiting Indians but eventually succumbed to the strength of Kazakhstan's forwards, ably led by skipper Timur Mashurov.

The Africa zone commenced with two surprises. Senegal, in their first RWC outing, hammered fellow RWC newcomers Nigeria 46-6 in Dakar, while Swaziland surprised their enthusiastic coach and union president, Mike Collinson, with a narrow 24-23 win over their visitors from Zambia. Senegal continued their winning campaign, collecting in succession the scalps of Cameroon and Zambia in this preliminary stage, before succumbing to the superior firepower and experience of former RWC finalists Zimbabwe and Côte d'Ivoire in round one proper. Côte d'Ivoire as pool

winners pass through automatically to round two along with Kenya, who topped the other round one pool, while Zimbabwe and Uganda fight it out in a play-off for the final spot in the round that brings onto the scene the continent's heavyweights – Namibia, Tunisia and Morocco.

The latest zone to kick off was Oceania, in late June 2005. Even so, the winners and runners-up in the three-team Section A of the draw, Samoa and Fiji, have already emerged and qualified for the RWC finals as Oceania 1 and Oceania 2. The third-placed side, Tonga, will re-enter the fray against the winners of Section B, which includes all the island nations – Tahiti, Niue, Papua New Guinea, Solomon Islands, Vanuatu and Cook Islands. The winners of this Oceania play-off will play in the Repechage against the runners-up of the Asia zone.

ABOVE Spain on the offensive during their 63-9 defeat of Hungary in Madrid in round two. Spain topped their group and passed through to round three.

FACING PAGE A Polish put-in in Gdynia, where the home side ran out 20-15 victors over Switzerland. The Poles are in the same round three pool as Spain.

BEHIND SCOTTISH RUGBY.

THE
FAMOUS
GROUSE
SCOTLAND TEAM SPONSOR

Summer Round-up 2005

by GRAHAM CLUTTON

'After Wales had softened up the North Americans, England travelled west to compete in and subsequently win the Churchill Cup.'

aving won a first Grand Slam in 27 years earlier in the year, Wales provided further confirmation of their rugby resurgence under Mike Ruddock with resounding back-to-back victories against the USA and Canada on their summer tour to North America. Although Wales set off across the Atlantic without a good many of their Six Nations Championship-winning squad (due to injury or Lions duty, to the latter of which they also later lost Ryan Jones), the Dragons

were far too good for their hosts. They defeated the USA Eagles 77-3 in Hartford, Connecticut, and followed up with a 60-3 success against the Canadians in Toronto.

Ruddock's men ran in 11 tries without response against the Eagles, with Ceri Sweeney, having switched to centre from outside half, notching up a 100 per cent record with his boot by slotting all 11 conversions. Just five players remained from the Wales side that clinched the Grand Slam against Ireland at the Millennium Stadium back in March: Kevin Morgan, Adam Jones, Brent Cockbain and Ryan Jones were all included in a side that was led by Mark Taylor on his 50th appearance for his country.

Llanelli Scarlets hooker Matthew Rees made his debut at the Rentschler Field Stadium, an American Football venue, while Blues winger Craig Morgan made his first start since France back in 2003. The Eagles managed only one penalty, from Mike Hercus. Ruddock made the most of his side's dominance by handing Ben Broster his debut from the replacements' bench, on a night that highlighted the gulf between the two nations.

Seven days later, and with Ryan Jones having left for New Zealand on the eve of the game, Wales's young guns kept the heat on Ruddock's missing stars with a scorching performance to see off Canada 60-3 in the searing sun of Toronto's York Stadium. Indeed, it was the performance of his side's wealth of newcomers that left coach Ruddock smiling, as debutant teenage winger Chris Czekaj and rookie prop Broster both grabbed tries in the near 100-degree heat.

Captain Taylor got the ball rolling as he finished off a well-worked Welsh move on 14 minutes to add to Ceri Sweeney's earlier penalty. Although Canada full back Derek Daypuck managed to open the hosts' scoring with a 17th-minute penalty, Wales reasserted their authority and chalked up another significant success.

Ruddock hailed the six debutants, who fitted in well to the Grand Slam champions' style during the two record-breaking wins. He said, 'It was a tougher battle than the USA, the pitch was narrower, there was a lot of wind around and they were a tough team. They were well drilled and they fronted up in the first half.

LEFT Wales scrum half Mike Phillips is caught by the USA Eagles defence during the clash in Hartford, Connecticut.

PAGE 71 A familiar sight in North America and New Zealand in the summer of 2005: Ryan Jones on the charge, this time against the Eagles before he was called to Lions colours.

ABOVE Wendell Sailor of the Barbarians escapes England's Hugh Vyvyan.

LEFT England's Tom Voyce gets the ball away in the Churchill Cup final despite the attentions of two Pumas.

'But we took control straightaway and we came through it. It wraps up what has been a very positive tour for us – we've given out six new caps, scored well over 100 points and not conceded a try and that just shows the desire and team spirit we have here.

'What pleases me is that whenever we bring in a new player they slot right into the system. Scott Johnson has been brilliant with the skills and all the young players have benefited from being around the senior players.

'Considering we had 11 players away, the boys coming through have been superb and it shows what we've got in this squad.'

After Wales had softened up the North Americans, England travelled west to compete in and subsequently win the Churchill Cup. Having beaten Canada 29-5 in the semis, the England A team beat Argentina 45-16 in the final, with Wasps full back Tom Voyce running in two tries as England made light work of the Pumas in Edmonton. James Simpson-Daniel, Paul Sackey and Andy Gomarsall also crossed as the tourists reclaimed the crown they lost to New Zealand Maori last year. Leicester fly half Andy Goode missed just one of six attempts at goal but was sent to the sin bin for the second match in succession.

Captain Pat Sanderson was delighted with the result and said: 'Winning is massively important. Every time you play, you play to win.' A crowd of 17,000 watched the final and Sanderson added: 'It's very important that the Canadian public get to see international teams and high-level performances from athletes.'

England did, however, lose a non-cap match against the Barbarians at Twickenham by 52-39 on 28 May despite fielding ten full caps in their starting line-up. However, only Jamie Noon had started against Scotland in the Calcutta Cup match in March, while Andy Goode and Mike Worsley had been replacements. Paul Sackey (2), Ayoola Erinle, Pat Sanderson and replacement James Forrester

crossed for tries; Goode added ten points with the boot, and his replacement, Sam Vesty, converted twice. The Barbarians tries came from Wendell Sailor (2), Bruce Reihana (2), Brent Russell (2), Carlos Spencer and South Africa centre Trevor Halstead. Reihana converted six of them to round off a classic BaaBaas game.

Ireland, who had been disappointing in the Six Nations Championship, played two Tests in Japan on 12 and 19 June, winning both under the captaincy of David Humphreys, who has now won 69 caps. In the first Test at Osaka, Ireland won 44-12, with Humphreys kicking a conversion and two penalties before leaving the field to be replaced by Jeremy Staunton, who landed two conversions and four penalty goals. Tries came from wing Tommy Bowe, centre Kevin Maggs, hooker Frankie Sheahan and prop Simon Best.

LEFT Flanker Kelly Brown, in his first game for Scotland, against the Barbarians at Aberdeen, hands off to the waiting Mike Blair (No. 9).

FACING PAGE Mike Blair tracks Romania's Razvan Mavrodin during Scotland's 39-19 victory in Bucharest.

The Irish handed out first caps to No. 8 Roger Wilson and lock Matt McCullough, both of whom started the game, and also to four replacements – hooker Bernard Jackman, lock Trevor Hogan, scrum half Kieran Campbell and centre David Quinlan.

In the second Test in Tokyo, Ireland won 47-18, with Humphreys converting six of the seven tries and touching down for one of his own. Other tries went to Sheahan (2), centre Gavin Duffy (2), flanker David Wallace and full back Girvan Dempsey, who was winning his 60th cap. A further new cap was replacement centre Kieran Lewis.

Scotland, who won just one championship game – against Italy – played a non-Test match against the Barbarians on 24 May at Aberdeen, captain Jon Petrie leading them to a 38-7 victory. The starting line-up included uncapped players Kelly Brown at blind-side and Scott Lawson at hooker. Chris Paterson, playing at full back, kicked five conversions and added a penalty; tries came from centre Andrew Henderson, wing Sean Lamont, prop Allan Jacobsen and two replacements – Hugo Southwell and Douglas Hall. Prop Euan Murray and flanker Andrew Wilson, both also uncapped, came on as replacements. David Humphreys led the Barbarians and converted prop Andrea Lo Cicero's try.

Scotland then travelled to Bucharest and on 5 June beat Romania 39-19 in front of 2800 spectators. Paterson won his 56th cap and Scott Murray his 68th as Petrie led a side that saw Brown and Lawson start as new caps and score. Paterson, Murray, Henderson and Dan Parks all also scored tries, while Paterson added three conversions and a penalty.

HOME FRONT

Bristol's Second Coming

by ALASTAIR HIGNELL

'Hill admits that playing rugby Bristol-fashion means taking risks and that risk-taking and Premiership survival are uneasy bedfellows.'

On Easter Sunday 2005, Bristol thrashed nearest rivals Exeter at the Memorial Ground to guarantee their Second Coming. Promotion meant that the West Country outfit became the first team in the modern era to have twice fought their way back into the top flight. And they did it a year ahead of schedule. 'Our aim was to finish third,' admits head coach Richard Hill. 'After finishing ninth the previous season, we intended to be competitive this season, and be ready for promotion at the end of year three.'

Bristol are not only glad to be back where they belong – since their formation in 1886 until their temporary demise in the professional era, the club have always been one of the powerhouses of the English game – but are determined to light up the Premiership with the style of rugby that returned them to the big time.

In winning 22 of their 26 first division matches, Bristol ran up 940 points, 135 more than their nearest rivals. In the Powergen Cup, they held Wasps to a 33-33 draw at the end of normal time. In their other matches in front of the national television cameras, they performed heroically against Gloucester at Kingsholm and sublimely in that title decider against Exeter.

'We play fifteen-man rugby,' claims Hill. 'We want to keep the ball alive, use it before contact, and out of contact; we want to stay on our feet and develop the free-flowing style that we see in the Heineken Cup from Toulouse, Stade Français and Biarritz, but is so different to the sort of game we see in the Premiership.'

Hill admits that playing rugby Bristol-fashion means taking risks and that risk-taking and Premiership survival are uneasy bedfellows. However, his faith is shaped not just by a romantic desire to see more exciting rugby but by Bristol's experience last season.

'We radically changed our style of rugby over the summer. We'd signed some experienced forwards like Darren Crompton, Ed Pearce, Matt Salter and Jim Brownrigg, so felt we could build a game plan based on more than the 30 per cent possession that had been our rations the year before. But we fell three tries behind to Penzance on day one, trailed London Welsh at half-time in our first home match and squandered any number of chances in losing at home to Plymouth, before we could truthfully have confidence in a new way of playing.'

Defeat by Plymouth was followed by 11 wins in a row in league and cup rugby, a surge to the top of the table – and that extraordinary cup clash with Wasps. By now, the national media had come to call, and to ask whether Bristol were ready for the top flight and, were they to finish top, whether they believed that the powers that be would contrive to prevent their promotion.

Publicly, Bristol declared their belief that they met all the criteria necessary for promotion. Behind the scenes, chief executive John Portch prepared two budgets – one to cater for life in the Premiership, the other for the next season's scheduled promotion push. Hill and his coaching staff were equally cautious. 'We may have been

LEFT Josh Lewsey of Wasps can't stop Bristol centre Rob Higgitt as he powers away to score his team's second try of their Powergen sixth round tie. Tied 33-33 after normal time, the match ended 43-33 to Wasps.

top but we knew we still had our hardest fixtures ahead of us – two matches against Exeter, away to Plymouth, our last three matches away from home. We reckoned that we should switch our target from finishing third, but we still didn't aim higher than second.'

New Year results suggested that they were only being realistic. Wasps' disqualification from the Powergen Cup gave Bristol an unexpected extra day in the limelight – at Kingsholm in the rain, with playing resources already stretched thin. The knowledge that Pertemps Bees had seen their league season implode when faced by similar cup distractions the year before resonated even more warningly as defeat at Kingsholm was followed by a heavy loss to Exeter, an unexpected reverse at home to Penzance, Powergen Shield defeat at Plymouth and injuries to key players.

But just as the year-two target became more and more achievable, so did the ultimate goal of promotion become more compromised. A big-spending heavyweight – at that stage either Northampton or Harlequins – looked likely to come down from the Premiership, while other clubs in the first division were rumoured to be accumulating financial resources well beyond the reach of a Bristol club that had twice gone close to bankruptcy in the past decade.

'One of the directors, Rob Clilverd, came up to me and said, "We really need you to do it this year. Penzance and Exeter are going to have enormous clout next season, and the first division is going to be even more competitive than it is now." As a result, we called the players in, and even though the fixture list looked horrendous, agreed to increase our skills training sessions by 40 per cent and set a target of winning our last seven games.'

The board did its bit by funding the recruitment of high-quality reserves like Craig Short, Hentie Martens, Manuel Contepomi and Mark Woodrow. The supporters, who themselves had raised the money to sign full back Bernardo Stortoni earlier in the season, turned out in force – 10,000-plus flocked to the Memorial Ground for the Exeter game – and, with other results falling their way, the Shoguns only needed to win the first five.

And now the hard part – staying up. Bristol have been this way before when the millions of

RIGHT With Wasps disqualified for fielding a cup-tied player, Bristol got a Powergen quarter-final at Gloucester. The Shoguns put up a fight – here Gloucester's Seti Kiole comes a cropper – but the Cherry and Whites triumphed 21-0.

Malcolm Pearce bankrolled a Bob Dwyer vision; box office stars like Henry Honiball, Frank Bunce, Jason Little, Agustin Pichot and Felipe Contepomi strutted their stuff on the Memorial Ground and a place in the Heineken Cup was secured. Then, with just as bewildering speed Pearce withdrew his backing, relegation followed, the stars dispersed and Bristol had to build again from rock bottom.

There's no desire for a return to the days of boom and bust. The post-Pearce board includes former playing legends Nigel Pomphrey and Alan Morley, as well as savvy businessmen Clilverd and Portch; all are determined to retain the ethos of a community club without overreaching into a soulless corporate world. Hill and his players are more than happy to buy into the philosophy.

'I was brought up on the idea of the rugby club as the heart of the community. It's not a question of the playing side, the corporate side and, by the way, the supporters. We have a very loyal set of supporters and it is important to have a dialogue with them. The Supporters Club contribution in paying Bernardo Stortoni's salary was a key factor in our success, and I think it is vital that our players interact positively with the community.'

Hill therefore approached his summer recruitment campaign with a template for the type of player he was after. Leeds, England and Lions hooker Mark Regan is a Bristolian, while centre Mark Denney also returns to the club. Former Sale full back Vaughan Going originates from North Auckland, where rugby is central to the community. The same is true of Wales's most-capped forward Gareth Llewellyn.

They join a squad that is brimful of ambition; players like Joe El Abd, Sean Marsden, Sam Cox and Rob Higgitt all have points to prove after failing to make a big enough impact first time around. Argentina internationals Manuel Contepomi and Bernardo Stortoni are quality attacking players.

And, according to Hill, attack is top of the agenda. 'We'll be under pressure to start well, and we could do it by using our forwards to smash it up the middle, play for territory, kick and chase. But I'm convinced the only way for this club to go is to show faith in the fifteen-man vision. We may have early disappointments, but I'm convinced that if we stick to our guns, we'll start to earn the results, playing the sort of rugby not often seen in the Premiership.'

Brave words, bravely spoken. Rugby fans of all persuasions will hope they bear fruit.

BELOW Bristolian, and former England hooker, Mark Regan returns to the Shoguns from Leeds Tykes for 2005-06.

Tykes Upset the Odds
the 2005 Powergen Cup Final
by ALASTAIR HIGNELL

'The increasingly composed Ross opened up the Bath defence and placed an inch-perfect chip for centre Chris Bell to gather and force his way over close to the posts.'

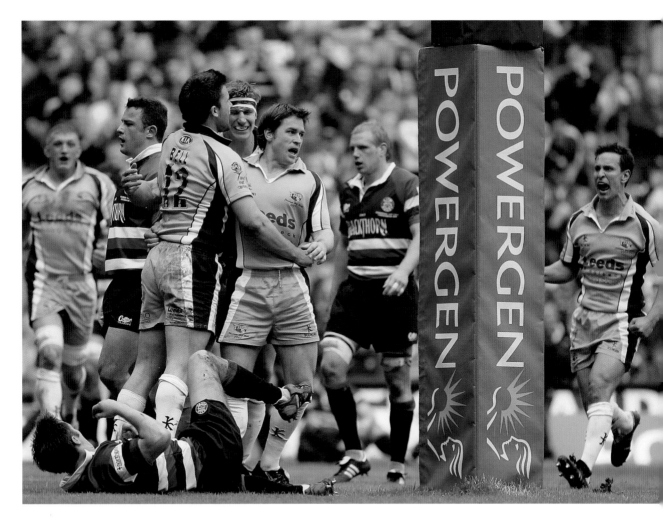

In winning the Powergen Cup for the first time in their history, Leeds displayed some of the best characteristics of the English game; they were mean and magnificently managed in defence, they took their chances well and refused to contemplate defeat. In losing for the first time ever in a Cup final, Bath displayed some of the worst features of the Premiership game; they were wooden, one-paced and desperately predictable. They never looked like scoring a try, and they deserved to lose.

Strength in teamwork

Clifford Chance is pleased to support Wooden Spoon.

Our mission is grounded in the belief that we have a responsibility as a business
to contribute to our communities. For further details see our website:
www.cliffordchance.com/community

Clifford Chance Limited Liability Partnership

C L I F F O R D
C H A N C E

www.cliffordchance.com

The current Bath outfit is cut from a very different cloth to the predecessors who won ten knockout titles in fourteen years from the early 1980s to the mid-1990s. In the likes of Jerry Guscott, Simon Halliday and Tony Swift, those teams could boast some of the greatest attacking talents of their generation, and played to them. New model Bath may be every bit as powerful as their forebears, but they are nowhere near as creative.

But they arrived at Twickenham as favourites. Riding high in the league, they were returning to the arena where only the year before they had contested the Zurich Premiership final. And their Cup form was good. After a routine romp against Harlequins, they had a one-point quarter-final victory at Sale and a last-gasp win at Gloucester in the semi-final that suggested they still had the appetite for the big knockout occasion.

Leeds by contrast were propping up the Premiership and had never been to Twickenham before. Although they hammered Pertemps Bees 81-17 in the sixth round, neither a hard-fought 24-19 quarter-final win at Northampton nor an equally unremarkable 15-6 win in a home quarter-final against London Irish suggested that they were arriving at Twickenham with more expectation than hope.

And they got off to the worst possible start when captain Iain Balshaw was forced off with a leg injury in the first three minutes. It was later revealed that Balshaw had damaged his quad muscle earlier in the week, but so keen to play against his former club, so keen to extend the run of form that had seen him named that week in the Lions squad, he gambled and failed.

Less than 25 minutes later, another of Leeds's major attacking weapons, Phil Christophers, was also out of the match, with damaged ribs. That, though, was as bad as it got for the Tykes. True, they did fall behind to an early Chris Malone penalty, but then two great strikes from Scottish international outside half Gordon Ross for a 6-3 advantage to Leeds suggested that this might be the day of the underdog.

After a scintillating counterattack launched against the run of play from inside their own half, Leeds could have

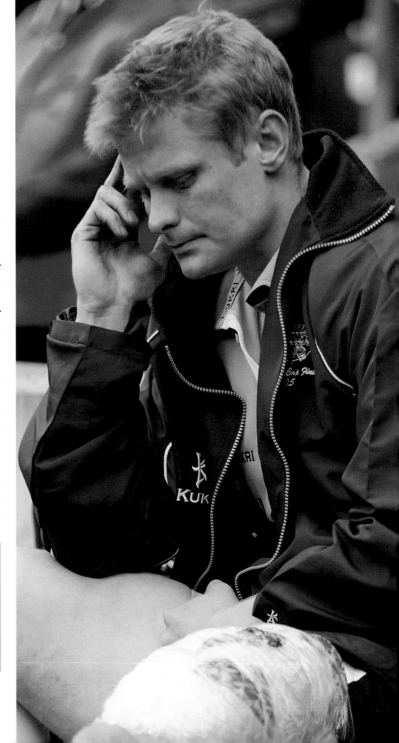

RIGHT A crestfallen Iain Balshaw sits out the remainder of the final with a recurrence of a quad injury that not only put him out of the match within three minutes of the start but also out of the Lions tour to New Zealand.

PAGE 85 Leeds players rush to congratulate Chris Bell, who has just crashed over for his side's first try.

scored the first try of the match but prop Mike Shelley made a hash of an overlap on the left. On the half-hour, they made no mistake when the increasingly composed Ross opened up the Bath defence and placed an inch-perfect chip for centre Chris Bell to gather and force his way over close to the posts.

Bath worked their way back into contention in the expected way – keeping the ball close to the forwards, chancing little with ball in hand, forcing their way into positions from which Malone could kick his goals. No one was surprised, or particularly excited, as the outside half obliged with two more penalties.

But Malone, and Bath, contrived to undo all their previous hard work when the Australian flung out a speculative long pass on the Leeds 22 and watched in horror as Tykes wing Andre Snyman intercepted and raced away from 70 metres out to score under the posts. Instead of going into the interval at 13-9 and closing, Bath were 20-9 down and flailing.

Malone did land another penalty five minutes after half-time and hit a post from 50 metres, but from there on in Bath grew ever more desperate in attack, while Leeds became ever more clinical in defence.

As Bath managed to butcher an overlap on the left with a quarter of the match to go, Malone missed a penalty which might have calmed frayed nerves. Leeds No. 8 Alix Popham intervened brilliantly to steal Bath possession on the Tykes try line, while Snyman managed to snuff out an attack from Matt Perry, Bath's only strike weapon on the day, with a superb smother tackle.

The final whistle, when it came, brought an end to a bizarre sort of stalemate. Bath, you felt, could have gone on for another couple of hours without really threatening to score a try. Leeds were hardly extended as they picked off some increasingly inept incursions.

The 20-12 result was greeted, as expected, joyously by Tykes supporters. Their season had not quite been turned on its head – they still needed Premiership victories over Harlequins and Bath to ensure that their Twickenham heroics would be rewarded by Heineken Cup rugby next season.

Also as expected, it was greeted by disbelief in the Bath ranks. Their hold on the knockout final had been broken – and in the worst possible way. In ten previous knockout finals, Bath had never failed to live up to the occasion, or the venue. Against Leeds, the big match temperament went missing. The fallout might be felt for some time to come.

While the one consolation for the West Countrymen was that their Cup record might never be broken, Leeds ended up as the last winners of the Powergen Cup in its present form. With the Welsh regions joining the competition – there will be four pools of four in October and December, culminating in the knockout stages in the spring – there could be an entirely new name on the trophy next April.

ABOVE Andre Snyman sweeps past Frikkie Welsh on his way to score Leeds's second try.

FACING PAGE Tom Biggs makes a spectacular challenge for a high ball against Bath's Olly Barkley.

OVERLEAF Leeds Tykes celebrate their first major trophy.

Sharks Attack
the 2005 Challenge Cup Final

by **TERRY COOPER**

'When Saint-André took over as the full-time rugby director at the start of the season, he set three goals – a high placing in the Premiership, entry into Europe and silverware.'

You've got to hand it to these Premiership coaches. Their loyalty to their players in terms of pushing them for honours – as opposed to contract negotiations – knows no boundaries. In the euphoria of winning the European Challenge Cup – the second-tier event – by mastering French team Pau at the Kassam Stadium, Oxford, Sale's rugby director, Philippe Saint-André, declared, 'I would choose all five of Sale's Lions for the Test matches against the All Blacks.'

Certainly Andy Titterrell (England's hooker playing on the flank), Mark Cueto, Andy Sheridan, Jason Robinson and Charlie Hodgson had a major influence in seeing off poor Pau in drenching conditions; Hodgson, Cueto and Titterrell scored all the points. Nevertheless Saint-André's enthusiasm was never going to be shared by the Lions coaches. Saint-André was on the mark, though, when he attributed the club's success – their second in the tournament in four seasons, continuing an England monopoly – to supremacy in the forwards, among whom prop Sheridan, a converted lock, was the cornerstone of the scrum. The pack created such a massive foundation and caused such relentless disruption that victory was as foreseeable as a result can ever be in a final. Pau had the humiliation of being shoved off their own scrum ball – and that's rare.

Saint-André highlighted Sheridan's display. 'Andy is getting better all the time. He's a very strong man, whose fitness is now where it should be. His discipline has also shown the necessary improvement.'

But he also amplified his admiration for the other Lions. 'Jason has got back to his best after his thumb injury that lost him Six Nations caps, while Cueto has been superb all season. Titterrell has proved his versatility by playing in the back row. Charlie showed that his confidence is back.

LEFT The immensely powerful Sebastien Chabal lays hold of Pau captain and flanker Pierre Som.

PAGE 91 Man of the Match Charlie Hodgson celebrates crossing the line for one of the tries that made up his haul of 17 points.

Even with such a vast Lions squad it's gratifying for a rugby director to have five of his squad taken on tour.'

Hodgson's round-the-field game was masterly, his goal-kicking in the tugging wind and rain merely mortal. 'I am confident in my game and all the Sale Lions hope that we can take this form into the tour. Yes, I missed half my kicks at goal. The conditions found me out, but I was striking the ball well.' All kickers from England's stable say that. The trick when it matters is to strike the ball well – and between the sticks.

BELOW Andy Titterrell, playing at flanker instead of in his usual position of hooker, crosses for Sale's second try of the final.

FACING PAGE Sharks skipper Jason Robinson and retiring scrum half Bryan Redpath lift the European Challenge Cup.

Saint-André was grateful to referee Alan Lewis for allowing Sale's power to enjoy its reward. 'Our set piece has been the key to us winning in Europe this season. For the Heineken and European Cups you need to be solid in that area. Pau are strong in the line out, but in the scrum and on the driving maul we smashed them. We were penalised out of the Premiership semi-final against Wasps. That doesn't happen in Europe, where referees let you scrum properly. It's important that good scrum teams are permitted to excel. Newcastle and Northampton struggled in the front five in the Heineken and lost heavily.'

Chris Jones – one of the varied back row that comprised his ball-handling and unique speed, Titterrell's sharpness and Sebastien Chabal's brute force – was also involved when Sale won this

competition in 2002. 'It's fantastic to have another trophy in the club's records. We wholly deserved it. We turned up in the right frame of mind and did the forward job we wanted and gave the backs the chance to control events.'

When Saint-André took over as the full-time rugby director at the start of the season, he set three goals – a high placing in the Premiership, entry into Europe and silverware. 'We have achieved all three. The Challenge win was England's only prize in the three Euro tournaments.'

Bryan Redpath ended his distinguished career in glory after five years at Sale. 'My final outing has been a marvellous send-off. I have my Scottish caps, but the two wins at Oxford will remain among my proudest moments.' He moves on to Saint-André's old club, Gloucester, where his knowledge will be utilised as backs coach.

The game flowed relentlessly Sale's way. Hodgson landed an early penalty from 30 yards. He then charged down a defensive kick and was fed the scoring pass for the opening try, converting superbly from touch. Pau's sole score came from Lionel Beauxis's penalty on the half-hour.

Six minutes later Cueto's powerful sprint was finished off by Titterrell, and Hodgson's conversion made it 17-3 at the interval. There were two long spells of the second half when Sale were denied, but in the 56th and 69th minutes more tries arrived. First Hodgson showed unexpected power with two hand-offs before offloading to Cueto, who claimed his 28th try of the season. Then the fly half scored his second try of the match after selling a dummy that baffled the Pau tacklers, bringing his contribution to 17 points and the final score to 27-3.

The Power of France
the 2005 Heineken Cup

by ALASTAIR HIGNELL

'Until two minutes from the end of normal time, however, Stade Français held the lead, and the belief that ... this might be second time lucky.'

The Power of Four – nifty slogan, lousy song – may have been coined to encapsulate the Lions assault on New Zealand, but as far as northern hemisphere club rugby is concerned, the only phrase in town is the Power of France.

When Toulouse ran out to face Stade Français in the Heineken Cup final, it was their third appearance in a row in this showpiece event and their fourth final in all. It was the second all-French final in three years, and although English clubs still have more individual titles, French domination of the knockout stages is becoming more pronounced by the year.

Three French clubs – Biarritz was the other – won their pools to earn home ties in the quarter-finals. All three won, with something to spare. Leicester, the last remaining team from outside the Republic, may have been good enough to deal with Irish top seeds Leinster, but they were crushed in their own city in the semi-finals.

Toulouse's defeat of the Tigers was memorably emphatic, and to English eyes horribly familiar. Leicester had suffered a similar fate in their home group game against Biarritz, while Gloucester's defeat at home to Stade Français was nothing short of humiliation. Newcastle were boys against men as they took on the same team in the Paris quarter-final. Northampton had been completely outclassed by Toulouse the day before.

And there's every chance that the gulf in class will grow ever wider. The old perception that French clubs were ambivalent about European rugby may have been given some credence by Bourgoin's embarrassing capitulation to Leinster, but the other clubs in France showed that when it comes to the Heineken Cup, they, and it, mean business.

Toulouse's triumph at Edinburgh ensured that seven of the newly reduced Top 14 will feature in next season's competition. It's no surprise that the same six who dominated the 2005 competition are back for more. Perpignan reached the Heineken Cup final only three years ago, while Biarritz made up for their semi-final defeat in Paris by winning the French title. Clermont, Castres and, to a lesser extent, Bourgoin all have form, and history, in Europe's premier competition.

They all know that success in Europe creates a virtuous circle. The better a team does on the big stage, the more sponsors and spectators it attracts. The more money that enters the coffers, the more a club can spend on its playing budget. The bigger the budget, the more star players a club can attract. The greater the strength in depth, the more chance the club has of success both in the National League and in Europe.

Toulouse therefore can attract something like 300 sponsors to generate a playing budget of over £10

FACING PAGE Toulouse fans lap up the sunshine during their team's Heineken Cup final victory over Stade Français at Murrayfield.

RIGHT Vincent Clerc congratulates Frédéric Michalak after he scores Toulouse's third try in their 27-19 semi-final win over Leicester at Welford Road. Austin Healey is suitably disgusted.

million. As a result they are able to offer state-of-the-art facilities and high salaries to encourage the likes of Wales skipper Gareth Thomas, French international Cédric Heymans and Irish forward Trevor Brennan to join the home-grown talents such as Frédéric Michalak and Benoit Baby. By the same token Stade Français have been able to lure proven international stars like Agustin Pichot and Juan Martin Hernandez to play alongside seasoned France players Christophe Dominici, David Auradou and Pieter de Villiers and up-and-coming talents such as Julien Arias and Rémy Martin.

And the final they produced at Murrayfield showed just how and why the French clubs have stolen a march on the rest of Europe. Although the match produced no tries, it was a feast of high intensity, high skill and high drama.

In the end it took a penalty and a dropped goal from Michalak in extra time to make sure that the cup was heading back to the Toulouse trophy cabinet. Until two minutes from the end of normal time, however, Stade Français held the lead, and the belief that, after defeat by Leicester in the 2001 final, this might be second time lucky. But Michalak's first penalty strike – the other points came from scrum half Jean-Baptiste Elissalde – levelled the contest, while another three-pointer in the first period of extra time took Toulouse ahead. The dropped goal that sealed success was opportunist, superbly executed – and late.

The first half was tense, perhaps reflecting the familiarity of old rivals shaping up to each other yet again. Toulouse had the best early chance, Gareth Thomas almost squeezing through after latching on to a beautifully weighted cross-field chip by Michalak. But Stade, powered by locks Mike James and David Auradou, gained the edge up front and took the lead in the 11th minute with David Skrela's first penalty. His second came just three minutes later, when Toulouse's forwards once again infringed at a ruck. By half-time the Paris marksman had kicked two more from a further two attempts, and with Elissalde on target with his two penalty attempts, Stade Français went into the interval 12-6 ahead.

The departure of France captain Fabien Pelous deprived Toulouse of their talismanic leader soon after half-time, but his replacement Jean Bouilhou inspired a renewed effort from his team-mates, and Elissalde's third penalty was a fair reflection of play. Wing Vincent Clerc then looked to have broken the deadlock, only to be hauled back by referee Chris White for a marginal forward pass, before Michalak set up the enthralling finish and Toulouse's greater big match experience pulled them through.

Toulouse had every right to ponder the value of their win when the draw for this season's competition lined them up against Wasps – their predecessors as Heineken Cup champions – as well as former semi-finalists Llanelli and Edinburgh. Stade Français also drew a short straw when they were grouped with seventh French club Clermont, former champions Leicester and the Ospreys.

Castres will fancy their chances of winning a group that also includes Sale, Munster and the Newport Gwent Dragons, while Perpignan should also finish top of a pool that features Leeds, Cardiff and Calvisano. Current French champions Biarritz should be too good for Saracens, Ulster and Benetton, while Bourgoin won't be overawed by last year's opponents Bath and Leinster, or by Glasgow.

Three French teams made it into the last eight of the 2005 Heineken Cup. That figure is likely to be even higher in 2006. As they sing in the Marseillaise, *Le jour de gloire est arrivé.*

FACING PAGE Olivier Sarramea, the Stade Français replacement scrum half, sets off on a sniping run at Murrayfield.

BELOW Toulouse wing Gareth Thomas tries to break Stade fly half David Skrela's tackle.

OVERLEAF Finau Maka on the balcony of Toulouse town hall as the Heineken Cup winners show off the trophy to their supporters the day after their 18-12 victory in Edinburgh.

SARACENS FOUNDATION
REGISTERED CHARITY No. 1079316

Sport for Health

ENHANCING THE LIVES OF CHILDREN & YOUNG PEOPLE THROUGH SPORT

To find out more about the work of the **Saracens Foundation** and how you can support visit **www.saracens.com** or call us on **01923 204 601**

REVIEW OF THE SEASON 2004-05

The Dragons' Tale
the 2005 Six Nations Championship by STEPHEN JONES

'But once again the attacking hammer was wielded chiefly by Shanklin in the centre. He seemed to find space at will in a crowded midfield.'

As the Welsh nation celebrated their Grand Slam at the end of the 1978 Five Nations Championship, there appeared to be no compelling reason why the long run of success for the great Welsh teams of that era should not continue. In any case, it would have been a thought to chill the blood of any nation if they had been granted fortune-telling powers and realised that it would be 27 years before their heroes were able to Slam again.

BELOW A determined Gavin Henson and Stephen Jones after the latter's 72nd-minute dropped goal in Wales's remarkable comeback in Paris.

It is difficult to even attempt to draw a veil over a period of that length, and of such sporting grimness. It is difficult enough to look back on those 27 years and try to judge which was the lowest point, simply because there are so many contenders for the title. It did seem, occasionally, that rugby was even drifting away from the hearts of the Welsh people.

It was not, of course. Some things run deeper than poor results. Wales won a quite magnificent Grand Slam in the RBS Six Nations Championship of 2005, not only dominating the European rugby scene but playing rugby of such verve and entertainment value that neutrals were dragged into their orbit to celebrate alongside delirious Welshmen.

Wales had been playing sparkling rugby in the years before this new Grand Slam, notably when they opted for all-out attack against New Zealand in their final pool match of the 2003 World Cup, and notably again when they once more ran New Zealand close in the autumn international series at the end of 2004. Yet on those occasions Wales still lacked real ringcraft, an established forward base and their defence could often be porous.

When Mike Ruddock took over as national coach for the season, he immediately set about strengthening the base. As the 2005 tournament was to show, he uncovered and unleashed a major new talent in Gethin Jenkins, the loose-head prop whose appearances had been rather fitful in the previous era, notwithstanding his talent.

There were to be other significant bonus points for Wales during the season, in particular in the advance of Brent Cockbain, the second-row who battled back wonderfully after family tragedy to become arguably the best lock in the tournament. Furthermore, Martyn Williams, the veteran flanker, was to produce stunning form in his inimitable and skilful style.

Behind the scrum, Ruddock ended any speculation about the career, future and playing position of Gavin Henson by immediately installing him at inside centre, reaping a vast reward in terms of a magnificent all-round game. Gareth Thomas was chosen as Ruddock's captain, and a likely half-back partnership of Stephen Jones and Dwayne Peel was selected to take Wales into the first match of their Six Nations campaign, against England at Cardiff. The partnership was to see out the season in grand style and to be reunited in the Lions Test team at the end of the season.

There was one more change made to the side, in the very week before the England game. Sonny Parker, the centre, suffered injury and Ruddock decided to install Tom Shanklin, of Cardiff Blues, alongside Henson. Shanklin had always been something of a peripheral figure for Wales. However, his arrival as a starting outside centre was to prove one of the most significant aspects in the transformation of the Welsh team from attractive losers to attractive winners.

Wales began with a win of massive significance over England. As events were to prove, the 11-9 victory came after what was, by a distance, the worst of their five performances leading to the Grand Slam. However, it is easy to make such observations with hindsight. England's recent dominance over Wales had been so absolute that a second string was able to win in Cardiff with ease in a 2003 World Cup warm-up match. England were denuded by injury and odd selection, but they were still the mental hurdle which Wales had to leap before they could even begin to establish themselves.

Yet Wales did score a real pedigree try in the first half, with a series of battering attacks ending with long, high passes across the midfield and a try in the corner for Shane Williams, the diminutive wing who was to prove another of the team's signature players. Despite their convincing superiority, Wales still trailed 9-8 as injury time approached, with Charlie Hodgson of England having kicked three penalties against the try by Williams and a penalty by Stephen Jones.

But when Wales were awarded a penalty in the dying moments, near halfway and way out on the right, there was no mistaking the crowd favourite to take the shot. Henson had played a stunning game, with his thunderous tackling upsetting Mathew Tait, the young English centre, who had an uncomfortable afternoon. Henson, with his customary self-confidence, almost begged to be given the responsibility of that fateful kick, and he drilled over a wonderful and nerveless goal. The celebrations were long and loud and Wales were on the road.

They were able to demolish Italy 38-8 in their next match, with a performance that was a tribute to their own pace and ambition against a team who had looked impressive in defeat at the hands of Ireland the previous week. The likes of Shane Williams and Gareth Thomas, and even the likes of Cockbain and Michael Owen in the forwards, showed electric footballing ability. There were three tries before half-time, from Jonathan Thomas, Martyn Williams and Tom Shanklin, against one from

ABOVE Scott Murray is tackled by Santiago Dellape in Scotland's 18-10 victory over Italy at Murrayfield.

FACING PAGE Jamie Noon runs at Chris Paterson on the way to scoring the second of his three tries for England as they beat Scotland 43-22 at Twickenham.

Luciano Orquera; and although Roland De Marigny landed a penalty at the start of the second half, Wales took complete command with further tries from Shane Williams, Cockbain and Robert Sidoli.

'Our forwards did well against what was one of the best packs in the tournament,' said Martyn Williams afterwards. Williams was made Man of the Match for his omnipresent performance, although as it turned out, things were to get better and better for the tenacious Cardiff flanker, and for his team.

Granted, it did not appear so as Wales went in 15-3 down at half-time in a brilliant match against France in Paris. In the early stages, France had been irresistible, and Dimitri Yachvili scored a try which he converted himself. There was another score from Aurélien Rougerie, and with some kicks from Yachvili the half-time lead was set up. Wales, who had hinted at attacking potential, appeared to be on the point of defeat, especially when Gareth Thomas, the captain, failed to re-emerge after half-time, having suffered a thumb injury which would keep him out of the remainder of the campaign.

However, if Wales were daunted, they did not show it. They made an amazing comeback. Martyn Williams scored after brilliant approach work from Stephen Jones and Shane Williams. Martyn Williams then scored again after another surging Welsh attack, diving over for his second try in three minutes to give Wales an incredible lead. Wales still led by six points towards the end, after Stephen Jones had kicked his third penalty and dropped a goal. But it was in these closing stages that a new and astonishing Welsh defensive resolution showed itself. The final score was 24-18. It had been an outstanding match, vivid and colourful, and it had lifted the whole tournament. But more than anything, it had shown that the Welsh revival was on firm foundations.

Scotland discovered this to their high cost when Wales went to Murrayfield for the fourth leg. By this time, the giant and athletic figure of Ryan Jones was installed on the blind-side flank and front-row forwards such as Mefin Davies and Adam Jones were discovering themselves in the heat of battle. Peel, moreover, was by now regarded as the outstanding scrum half in the championship.

But even allowing for these matters, the Welsh start was sensational. By a bewildering mixture of brilliant attack and counterattack and finishing of deadly precision, Wales scored tries in the fourth, tenth, fourteenth and twenty-seventh minutes. The tries came from Ryan Jones, the darting Rhys Williams, Shane Williams and Kevin Morgan. The last-mentioned was outstanding in his attacking running from the back, making light of the absence of Gareth Thomas.

Morgan had scored again by half-time and Rhys Williams took Wales well into the forties with another score early in the second half. Wales did allow Scotland a few consolation tries late on, with Rory Lamont and Chris Paterson crossing for a final score of 46-22. There was definitely a looseness about the match, but the Welsh attacking play was devastating and was distinguished by the ability of Shanklin to cut the midfield defence to pieces with a bewildering variety of angles and powerful bursts.

Wales, staggeringly, had not beaten Ireland in Cardiff since 1983, surely the most inexplicable run in the whole of rugby history. Ireland's own aspirations to a Grand Slam had been crushed by a defeat at the hands of France, but they were intent on rescuing their season when they came to Cardiff for what turned out to be the greatest day in Welsh rugby history for nearly three decades, and possibly for more.

The Millennium Stadium was seething with excitement and passion. So was the nation outside. Wales won 32-20, their superiority in a compelling match was even greater than the scoreboard suggests, and by the end of the game the stadium appeared to be awash with champagne and tears of joy.

Wales were set on the way when Gethin Jenkins, who had already made some outstanding tackles, raced up to charge down a kick by Ronan O'Gara, then ran on to control the ball under pressure and score. Successful kicking by Stephen Jones and Henson took Wales well clear, and they were decidedly unlucky not to score a bagful of tries after the inspired prompting of Shane Williams and Stephen Jones and surges around the fringes launched by Owen and Peel.

But once again the attacking hammer was wielded chiefly by Shanklin in the centre. He seemed to find space at will in a crowded midfield. As the third quarter ended, Owen drove the ball on from a line out, Stephen Jones and Shanklin conspired in the midfield and launched Shanklin clean through. Morgan came up outside with the perfect supporting run, Shanklin found his man and the try at the posts, plus the conversion, made it 29-6 with 20 minutes to go, and all the tension could dissipate into celebration.

Geordan Murphy and Marcus Horan did cross for Ireland, but there was absolutely no way that Wales would be denied. They received the RBS Six Nations Championship Trophy, with the injured Gareth Thomas returning to join his colleagues for the presentation.

RIGHT Kevin Morgan crosses for his side's second try at the Millennium Stadium and Wales can breathe easy – Ireland will not catch them now.

As it turned out, the new self-confidence of the Welsh players was one of the few bright spots on the Lions tour. Certainly, the whole Welsh squad plus coaches will be avidly looking forward to a return with the All Blacks in Cardiff in November. But of more significance was the confirmation that Welsh rugby, at least at the very top, is restoring itself; and further good news came with a Grand Slam achieved by the Wales U21 team. Suddenly, in terms of spectator numbers and commercial income, the whole scene had been transformed. But especially in terms of sport, it was one of the Grandest Slams.

The Club Scene
England: Wasps' Zurich Treble

by **BILL MITCHELL**

'The Powergen Cup provided some superb fare, not least the semi-final between Gloucester and Bath. This match went to extra time and a late deciding try ...'

The 2004-05 season was an anomaly as far as the national team was concerned, with three of the five Six Nations matches lost – all by small margins – and, on paper at least, few signs that the younger players were superior to the kind of international opposition that can be expected in the future, since the U21s underperformed not only in their Six Nations games but also in the World Championship in Argentina. On the credit side the U19s were Grand Slam winners, but the overall picture is less encouraging than it should be.

The November matches against touring sides produced a massive success against Canada (70-0) and a convincing victory over South Africa (32-16) before some missed kicks by Hodgson (otherwise a very good player) saw defeat by Australia (19-21). Prospects for the remainder of the season looked good.

Indeed, as far as the main event – the Six Nations – was concerned, the team was in reality inferior only to Wales, who deservedly won with virtually the final kick of the game against England. This was a just

ABOVE Mark Van Gisbergen of Wasps races away to score in the Zurich Premiership final, urged on by a bloodied Joe Worsley.

FACING PAGE Martin Johnson looks on as Wasps players celebrate at the end of the Zurich Premiership final. There was to be no fairy-tale ending for Jonno, his Leicester side going down 39-14 at Twickenham in his last competitive match.

ABOVE Bedford's Ben Lewitt steps on the gas during his side's 14-13 win in the Powergen Challenge Shield final at Twickenham.

FACING PAGE James Norris of Sheffield Tigers on the charge in the Powergen Junior Vase final against Solihull at Headquarters, won 30-13 by the Yorkshiremen.

result, made even more so by the fact that England should have been down to 14 men for the whole of the second half instead of only ten minutes of it. A yellow card was the penalty meted out to Danny Grewcock for a dreadful and reckless challenge, which brought on a scuffle and also a yellow card for retaliation for Gareth Thomas, the Welsh captain.

It might seem invidious to mention this affair, but Grewcock has a poor disciplinary record by any standards and had for some reason escaped a citing from Wasps for an alleged foul on Lawrence Dallaglio only a week earlier. This situation left the England coach, Andy Robinson, free to select him, while his subsequent Six Nations efforts earned him a Lions place – and more trouble when he was again cited, by New Zealand, for alleged foul play. He became the first Lion in history to be banished from a tour for field misconduct, but if chances are taken with men whose good behaviour on the field cannot be guaranteed, then criticism must be expected if something goes wrong.

Sir Clive Woodward must ask himself the rhetorical question of whether that risk was worth taking. Also he must ask himself whether he was right to cram the huge squad with players who had won a World Cup but were now 18 months older and to virtually ignore in his selections the fact that Wales were the Six Nations champions (although that is for another writer to analyse). One could question, too, the wisdom of selecting the courageous Wilkinson, who had been absent from the England team since his World Cup brilliance through persistent injuries but was still willing to take more than his fair share of heavy knocks, or Jason Robinson, whose domestic situation (a pregnant wife) meant that he was probably in the wrong frame of mind for such an arduous undertaking. Further, was Neil Back, in his late thirties, still capable of taking on the world's best (although by an irony he was serving a four-week suspension for violent play when the tour started)? Too many risks perhaps? One has seen many examples in more than one country where a coach's favoured and trusted friends have continued to be selected after they have passed their 'sell by' dates.

In any event after the defeat to Wales, England lost 17-18 to France at Twickenham after outscoring the opposition in terms of tries scored; they suffered once again through the normally reliable Hodgson having another off day with the boot. England went on to lose 13-19 in somewhat controversial circumstances in Dublin, where the referee had an 'iffy' match, before beating Italy comfortably 39-7 at Headquarters. They rounded off their championship with a 43-22 victory over

Scotland, whose first-half defence was almost non-existent, in a loose but entertaining match at Twickenham, in which many (but not Sir Clive) thought that the visitors' Chris Paterson had played well enough to earn a Lions place.

On the domestic scene, the Powergen Cup provided some superb fare, not least the semi-final between Gloucester and Bath. This match went to extra time and a late deciding try when it looked as if a sudden-death goals competition would be needed to decide the matter. In the Twickenham final itself, hot favourites Bath foundered on a marvellous Leeds defence. The Tykes overcame the misfortune of losing star full back Balshaw in the early stages and held out to win thanks to Gordon Ross, who had belatedly been preferred in the Scotland team to Dan Parks. Earlier on finals day, there had been wins for Sheffield Tigers over Solihull (30-13) in the Junior Vase and for Morley over Westoe (21-11) in the Intermediate competition, while Bedford had a narrow (14-13) victory over Plymouth Albion in the Shield.

RIGHT Colin Stephens, captain of the victorious Morley side, lifts the Powergen Intermediate Cup after their 21-11 win over Westoe in the final.

BELOW Replacement Ross Lavery, in his first Varsity Match, makes it to the line ahead of Cambridge full back Ufton to make Oxford safe in the 2004 MMC Trophy game at Twickenham.

Elswhere in the domestic competitions Leicester won the Zurich Premiership ahead of Wasps, who then beat them comfortably 39-14 in the final of the play-offs at Twickenham. This meant that like the *Weakest Link* losers, their hard-earned top spot left them with nothing. Bristol, meanwhile, won National One ahead of Exeter to regain their top-league spot.

In the Inter-Services, The Army (whose Fijian-dominated squad won the Middlesex Sevens at the start of the season) beat off stout Naval resistance to retain the title. The sailors also lost to the Royal Air Force, a rare success for the latter, who had suffered since the Rory Underwood days.

Both the men's and women's UAU titles went to Loughborough, whose men had earlier enjoyed a rare victory over Cambridge; however, the game against the Dark Blues was lost convincingly – they have only won the fixture once. In the Varsity Match the Light Blues twice led against a better team and had a chance in the second half to break the Oxford domination before a late try by substitute Lavery clinched the result. Devon won a thrilling County Championship final against Lancashire 22-16, perhaps to prove that there is still a place, particularly in the West Country, for this fine traditional competition.

The women's game in England is flourishing, with a national team that is only narrowly second best in Europe to France and an ever-improving club game. This year saw a thrilling National Cup final between Wasps and Saracens, the two strongest clubs, which the former won with a (literally) last-gasp try.

If one adds to all this the fact that Rosslyn Park continue to stage their hugely successful Schools Sevens week, then one can talk of a thriving game in England. So one hopes that rumours about rifts at Headquarters are nothing serious and if they are true that the protagonists will set aside personal ambition for the greater good of a game that is bigger than all of them.

You'll be converted

once you see how we go to the ends of earth and beyond to give you the best property advice in Scotland

Culverwell
PROPERTY CONSULTANTS

68-70 George Street, Edinburgh EH2 2LT, **e-mail:** alex@culverwell.co.uk **Web:** http://www.culverwell.co.uk
Edinburgh - call Alex Culverwell **(0131) 226 6611** Glasgow - call Drew Waddell **(0141) 248 6611**

Scotland: Tough at the Top

by ALAN LORIMER

'To say that Edinburgh, Glasgow and, especially, The Borders were playing with one arm tied behind their backs was perhaps understating the reality facing the professional sides.'

It was another season of struggling against the odds for Scotland's professional clubs and another season in which they failed to make any impact in either Celtic or European competitions. For fans north of the border it was further frustration, but there was a realisation that, with a new regime in place at Murrayfield, there may be a better future ahead.

To say that Edinburgh, Glasgow and, especially, The Borders were playing with one arm tied behind their backs was perhaps understating the reality facing the professional sides. For a start, the Scottish trio of

ABOVE Glasgow scrum half Graeme Beveridge looks around for support as the tackles come in from Edinburgh's Allan Jacobsen and Paul Boston during the December Celtic League clash at Murrayfield.

teams operated in a state of almost constant war with national team coach Matt Williams, whose insistence on holding an excess of training sessions for the Scotland team meant that club coaches were frequently left with little time for match preparation.

Moreover, the nonsensical idea of playing an extra autumn international match against Australia exacerbated the situation to the point that the soured relations between Williams and the club coaches became a matter of public concern.

The Williams war was, in itself, bad enough for the pro teams, but so too was the matter of funding. The Scottish Rugby Union, eager to reduce its debts by offloading the professional teams onto a mythical market, had denied the clubs the kind of cash needed to compete against top sides. At its worst, this tight-fisted and wholly misguided policy resulted in The Borders operating on a budget of under £1 million. Poverty in pro rugby rarely spells success.

A third factor militating against achievement was the undermining of the professional teams by the former SRU chief executive, Phil Anderton, who hinted strongly that The Borders would be gone by the end of the season and that buyers were being sought for Edinburgh and Glasgow. It was a debilitating diet of doubt; it was a climate of uncertainty. Little wonder, then, that results were underwhelming.

BELOW Stuart Moffat beats Jon Petrie's tackle to score against Glasgow at The Greenyards.

FACING PAGE Glasgow Hawks celebrate clinching the Premiership at Hawick.

Yet despite Glasgow finishing only mid-table in the Celtic League, one place ahead of Edinburgh, and the cash-strapped Borders understandably in last place, there were some good results amid the overall gloom. Glasgow, still seeking an optimum squad, had successes over Edinburgh, Ulster, The Borders (twice), Llanelli Scarlets,

Connacht and Cardiff, while Edinburgh had notable wins over Cardiff, Glasgow, Llanelli, The Borders and Leinster.

For The Borders, under new coach Steve Bates, the former England and Wasps scrum half, their lowly bottom place disguises some good performances, in particular wins against Cardiff, Edinburgh and Leinster at Netherdale together with a number of small-margin defeats.

In Europe neither Glasgow nor Edinburgh were able to qualify for the quarter-finals of the Heineken Cup, while in the European Challenge Cup, The Borders, after a far-too-easy start against the Portuguese side Coimbra, had their progress halted by Clermont Auvergne.

Of course, results are not always what matters most. What does is the development of potential international players. In this context there was proportionally greater success from The Borders, where rookie Kelly Brown proved himself worthy of international selection in the Scotland back row against Romania, full back Stuart Moffat resurrected his Scotland career, hooker Ross Ford earned a first cap and Andy Miller showed himself ready to challenge for the open-side flanker position.

Glasgow, too, can reflect on developmental success, with caps for winger Rory Lamont, hooker Scott Lawson and prop Euan Murray, and a return to the international scene for scrum half Graeme Beveridge. Edinburgh, meanwhile, the best-funded of the three sides, worked hard to achieve international success for outside half Phil Godman.

In Scotland the amateur game is still important to the extent of commanding press coverage on a par with the pro game. It's easy to understand why this is so, given the small number of pro teams and the close relationship between the top amateur teams and their professional counterparts. Arguably the top tier of the BT Premiership is the interface between professional and amateur, providing the proving ground for young aspirants and supplying players to the Celtic League clubs when needs arise. Moreover, in times when practical sport seems to be disappearing from the school curriculum at an alarming rate (at least in the state sector), it is the clubs who now have responsibility for teaching youngsters the skills of rugby and for arranging appropriate competition.

What is becoming clear at the top end of the amateur game is that demographic trends are tilting the balance hugely. No longer can Borders clubs like Hawick dominate year after year as they did in the early years of league rugby. Now, with a massive drift of young people to Edinburgh and Glasgow, which between them have eight universities, and a simultaneous decimation of traditional manufacturing in the south of Scotland, there is simply not the player pool in the Borders to compete with the city clubs.

ABOVE Former Boroughmuir
player and present Dundee
HSFP captain Lindsey Graham
hitches a lift with 'Muir prop
Ramin Mathieson in the final of
the BT Cup, won 39-25 by the
Edinburgh club.

No surprise, therefore, that the top three places in the BT Premiership were occupied by city clubs, Glasgow Hawks securing with comparative ease a second successive title and Heriot's and Boroughmuir trailing in the wake of the Anniesland club. Hawks have been transformed, by uncompromising coach Peter Wright, from an underperforming outfit into a hard-working side that knows how to win. Significantly, in an age when even amateur clubs spend money on importing overseas players, Hawks achieved their second championship success with a squad of home-based players, the pick of them being hooker Fergus Thomson, now a professional with Glasgow.

Heriot's looked championship winners after making a flying start, but once they lost outside half Anders Monro, the Goldenacre side lost composure and had to accept second-place status. Equally Boroughmuir, playing most of their home matches on a building site masquerading as a rugby ground during the Meggetland redevelopment programme, produced some exhilarating displays only to lack consistency over the season.

Among the Borders clubs, Melrose were the top finishers, in fourth place, and encouragingly are moving towards a home-produced team. Elsewhere, Biggar showed up well in their first foray into Premier One rugby, Aberdeen consolidated their position with a mid-table finish; but for Gala it was a quick return to Premier Two after a catastrophic season that suggests that a realignment of interests in the Borders leading to mergers may be imminent.

Promoted from Premier Two were Stirling County, the runaway winners of the second-tier competition, and Stewart's Melville, who have raised the number of Edinburgh teams in the top flight. Meanwhile, Boroughmuir atoned for their disappointing league season by winning the BT Cup with a 39-25 victory in the final over Dundee HSFP, whose runners-up status for a second consecutive season mirrored exactly the fortunes of their school side, defeated again by winners Dollar Academy.

Wales: Ospreys Celtic Champions

by DAVID STEWART

'Thus a solid platform was made available to a back line spearheaded by the other notable hairstyles of Messrs Henson and Shane Williams, which in turn was too good for all the other contenders; the Ospreys took the league title ...'

At the end of the 2003-04 season the WRU dropped a bombshell when the disbandment of the Celtic Warriors was announced. In keeping with tradition, this time round they almost torpedoed the Celtic League, when the Scots and Irish took umbrage at their cloak-and-dagger attempts to get into bed with the English neighbours in the form of a new cup competition that was going to occupy a chunk of the prime fixture slots. Only an embarrassing climbdown by the men at Welsh headquarters (and a bit of re-jigging of the league financials, not in favour of the Welsh you can be sure) restored a degree of harmony, if not trust.

So yet again the off-the-field stuff placed a diverting and wholly unnecessary cloud over the rugby itself, which is a pity as the Ospreys made a lot of progress; but truth be told they were the only region to do so. Year two of the new format saw the Scarlets stagnate, having lost a season of rebuilding, and the Dragons hold their own before probably regressing next term as cash shortfalls bite. Meanwhile, the Blues seem just to be a mess.

The merging of Neath and Swansea has been more seamless on the park than off it, but the bickering between two great old clubs will hopefully be minimised now with the move to a splendid new 20,000-seater stadium built by Swansea Council on the eastern side of the city (Neath is just across the estuary). Lyn Jones and Sean Holley did the smartest bit of recruitment of all when the Warriors went 'belly up', getting Sonny Parker, Brent Cockbain and Ryan Jones (the only player all the other regions were after). The first named missed a large chunk of the season through injury. However, the latter two, alongside the 'hair bear bunch' (Duncan and Adam Jones, who propped effervescent skipper Barry Williams throughout) and Jonathan Thomas plus a highly promising open-side in Richie Pugh provided the core

LEFT Richard Mustoe of the Ospreys holds up Edinburgh's Brendan Laney as Gavin Henson arrives in support during the Celtic League clincher at The Gnoll.

FACING PAGE Centre Tal Selley, who scored three tries in the game, leaves the Dragons' Sione Tuipulotu grasping at thin air during the Scarlets' 49-19 Celtic Cup quarter-final win at Rodney Parade.

PREVIOUS PAGE The Ospreys' captain Barry Williams hoists high the Celtic League trophy at The Gnoll.

to a pack that seems to be in the New Zealand mould – that is, having good set-piece basics allied to mobility and ball-handling skills.

Thus a solid platform was made available to a back line spearheaded by the other notable hairstyles of Messrs Henson and Shane Williams, which in turn was too good for all the other contenders; the Ospreys took the league title by seven points from Munster. It was clinched on a beautiful sunny Saturday evening in late March at The Gnoll – only a week after the Grand Slam had been secured at the Millennium Stadium – with a 29-12 win over an Edinburgh side who nobly came to chuck the ball around. A game suitable for a championship decider in an intoxicating atmosphere of celebration was the result. The Ospreys finished up appropriately a week later against Connacht in Galway, everybody's favourite party town of all the competition venues.

The coach made it immediately clear in the aftermath of victory that his sights now go higher, but the Heineken draw has done the Ospreys no favours – Stade Français, Clermont Auvergne and Leicester complete what will surely become tagged as this year's 'pool of death' (a metaphor sportswriters really ought to avoid, given some of the dangers of today's world). Jones was wry: 'If you want to win European cups you really have to go to France to win a game of rugby, and fortunately for us, we now have two opportunities!'

The Celtic Cup was shifted to the season's end, and it provided a freshness to contests at that stage, particularly in favourable weather and conditions. Sad to report, therefore, that the powers that be are doing away with it. Ulster certainly enjoyed their win in the inaugural one a year previously, and although the Scarlets lost 27-16 to Munster in the final at Lansdowne Road this year,

LEFT Former Newport captain and Harlequins assistant coach Paul Turner has taken over as head coach to the Dragons.

FACING PAGE Xavier Rush scores for the Auckland Blues against the Otago Highlanders during the 2005 Super 12. The former All Black has signed for Cardiff Blues for 2005-06.

they felt that reaching that point gave their fans some reward in an otherwise difficult time. A combination containing Robin McBryde, Vernon Cooper, Chris Wyatt and the wonderfully enduring John Davies is too long of molar to be effective at the top level these days. It also defies belief that Stradey, a ground that used to be a repository for some of the best flowing football anywhere, is still exposed to a battering ram like Salesi Finau behind the scrum. Eyebrows have been raised at their apparent willingness to recruit from overseas. True, lack of an effective No. 10 was a real problem last term, with neither Gareth Bowen nor Arwel Thomas filling the substantial gap left by Stephen Jones's departure to Clermont Auvergne. However, hiring the excellent Mike Hercus flies in the face of developing home talent, when someone like Ceiron Thomas showed up so well at the end of last season.

Gareth Jenkins, one of the nicest men in the game, eventually put his rejection by Wales behind him, and did much on the Lions tour to restore a reputation that was becoming a little battered in west Wales by the time Glasgow trounced the Scarlets 30–57 in their last home league game. A fifth-place finish, 30 points behind the Ospreys, was no good at all for local bragging rights. Nigel Davies and Paul Moriarty will continue to do the hands-on coaching, but it is the director of rugby who sets the tone. With the pace of Tal Selley and Matthew Watkins available in midfield, and hopefully a fit-again Mark Jones to join Barry Davies and Garan Evans in the back three, a return to running rugby is surely the way ahead.

The Dragons, with the flowing locks of Percy Montgomery to the fore, came a respectable fourth on 50 points. A season that started with Declan Kidney letting them down, to be replaced as an emergency measure by Chris Anderson (a bizarre experiment that predictably did not work out), never gathered any real momentum. The South African player and the Australian rugby league coach have both now departed, along with long-standing and long-suffering benefactor Tony Brown, and frankly, with belts being tightened all round, a turbulent period may well lie ahead.

Paul Turner is a sound choice for a team desperate for some stability following the loss of Mike Ruddock a year earlier. His status as a former Newbridge and Newport captain may give some much-needed impetus to embracing the Gwent region north of the M4, but the enthusiastic and knowledgeable former out-half, retreating from relegated Harlequins, may be facing his biggest challenge in a tracksuit. At least Michael Owen, Ian Gough and Peter Sidoli (younger brother of Robert) provide a line out, while Gareth Cooper, Ceri Sweeney and Kevin Morgan (may this most enterprising of players at last stay injury free) offer attacking options behind. Their last Heineken campaign stayed alive until the last pool round, when they came up short at Newcastle – amidst much unnecessary 'banter' from Rob Andrew in the week of the match – and a pool next time containing Sale, Castres and an ageing Munster is by no means the toughest.

Cardiff Blues require major surgery. They came ninth out of eleven teams, with only Connacht and the lowly Borders below them. What could be a powerhouse within the Welsh game merely limped into the Heineken by winning a play-off game at humble Viadana of Italy, after the Lions had left these shores. That meant the outstanding Martyn Williams, Gethin Jenkins and Tom Shanklin were all unavailable. And therein lies part of the problem. Their best three players are two from Pontypridd and an Anglo-Welshman. The failure to develop more talent from within the boundaries of the capital city – and now the most populous rugby region – over an extended period is a shocking indictment of their management and coaching. Whispers from those Warriors who joined up suggested the level of match analysis and tactical appreciation they found at their new place of employment fell below what they were used to.

Xavier Rush from Auckland is a signing who will bring footballing and leadership qualities, and to be fair, home-grown products are starting to flower in the form of Robin Sowden-Taylor at flank and exciting left wing Chris Czekaj, who was capped at 18 years of age against Canada in June. The Robinson brothers went missing last term through illness (Nicky) and injury (Jamie), so the future may just be a little brighter. A Heineken campaign of one win from six outings is not something the Arms Park faithful will tolerate again, and without bums on seats, the whole commercial edifice gets very shaky indeed.

Predictions? A still youthful and developing Ospreys squad to dominate again on the Celtic scene and give a good account in Europe; it is telling that Neath won the domestic Premier League title, so there is depth in the region. The other three are more likely to struggle, although if the Blues get their coaching right, they do have the players to be a surprise packet.

TRAVIS PERKINS FOR ALL YOUR CONVERSIONS

Gardens

Bathrooms

Lofts

Kitchens

No matter what you're looking to convert we can help – from complete renovations to finishing touches, like door handles and taps. Whatever you've got planned kick things off to a good start with a visit to Travis Perkins.

BUILDERS MERCHANTS
AWARDS
EXCELLENCE
2004
NATIONAL
BUILDERS
MERCHANT
OF THE YEAR
2004

PROUD SPONSORS OF NORTHAMPTON SAINTS

Travis Perkins

www.travisperkins.co.uk

Ireland: Munster Grab Celtic Cup

by SEAN DIFFLEY

'Sounds emanating from the IRFU proclaim the governing body's determination to help out the clubs, which they admit are the backbone of the game. But running the professional game ... leaves the union in a parlous financial state ...'

M unster saved Irish blushes after the disappointing failures in the Heineken Cup with a fine win in the final of the Celtic Cup, beating the Simon Easterby-led Llanelli at Lansdowne Road 27-16. It was the best match witnessed at the old ground in the season. Ronan O'Gara showed no signs of ring rust, revelling in his noted qualities of very fine line-kicking and precision passing. He contributed 17 points of Munster's total, going through the card – a try, a dropped goal, a penalty goal and three conversions.

Anthony Foley, the Munster captain, accepted the trophy. In his side were four who were to travel to New Zealand with the Lions – O'Gara, John Hayes, Paul O'Connell and Donncha O'Callaghan. And Foley can keep the Celtic Cup because that aspect of the competition will not continue. But the Celtic League remains in contention despite

ABOVE Llanelli Scarlets captain Simon Easterby cannot prevent Anthony Horgan of Munster from scoring his team's first try in the Celtic Cup final at Lansdowne Road. The Irish side emerged 27-16 winners.

a slight hiccup with the WRU, when plans for the Welsh clubs to participate in Anglo-Welsh events ruffled the feathers for a while of the Irish and Scots.

That Celtic Cup final was also the swansong for Munster's coach, the very popular – and successful – Alan Gaffney. It was an emotional farewell, as he and his family, after his spate of coaching with Leinster and then Munster, are returning to Australia, where Gaffney will be involved in a coaching role with the Wallabies.

The Heineken Cup final in Edinburgh was not quite devoid of an Irish interest, with the gregarious Trevor Brennan winning a second champion's medal with Toulouse. There had been talk that Clive Woodward was thinking about including Brennan in his Lions selection. But he didn't, and one wonders if that was yet another lapse in selectorial wisdom.

Declan Kidney, the coaching maestro when Munster had their best runs in the Heineken Cup, but who left to work with the Irish squad and then took over at Leinster, returns now to Munster. Leinster, flatterers only to deceive, have not lost Kidney alone – several players have decided to go abroad. Hooker Shane Byrne, left out of the Irish reckoning and the Leinster one, has signed up for Saracens, and Irish and Leinster lock Leo Cullen has departed for Leicester.

On the domestic club scene, an area now more amateur than ever, the clubs are finding the going difficult. Sounds emanating from the IRFU proclaim the governing body's determination to help out the clubs, which they admit are the backbone of the game. But running the professional game, paying the large salaries and other expenses of the four provinces and the Irish squad, leaves the union in a parlous financial state and limits what it can do for the clubs.

Still, the AIB-sponsored All Ireland League, organised in three divisions, had a successful season, and the decision to run the three finals at Lansdowne Road on the same afternoon was a successful move. It transpired that Shannon annexed their seventh title in 15 seasons, and Mick Galwey, in his first season as Shannon coach, suggests that he could be en route to a wider and higher role.

Shannon beat Belfast Harlequins 25-20 in the first division final, and the strange feature was that Shannon scored all their points in the first half to lead 25-0 at half-time. They failed to score in a second half that saw a plucky Harlequins with a never-say-die attitude get their 20 points with tries from Matt Mustchin, Ian Humphreys (younger brother of David) and Greg Mitchell.

Shannon's match-winning 25 points in the first half came from tries from centre Brian Tuohy, prop Nigel Conroy and flanker Colm McMahon. Out-half David Delaney added two conversions and two penalty goals. A great break through midfield gave Tuohy the opening try, Conroy burst over from a close maul and McMahon gained his score from a smart break from a scrum.

Humphreys, playing his last match for Harlequins before departing across the Irish Sea to Leicester, looked a very good young prospect. He kicked a penalty goal against Shannon and converted one try. Andy Thompson, who came on as a late replacement centre for Shannon, picked up his seventh league winner's medal – a quite remarkable feat.

UL Bohemians, also from Limerick, took the second division honours, ousting the Dublin club St Mary's College 18-12. However, the result didn't affect promotion as the season's work had already ensured that both were promoted to the first division for the new campaign.

Nevertheless UL Bohemians were particularly pleased, as they had been deprived of honours in the past two seasons, beaten in the finals

FACING PAGE Colm McMahon celebrates with team-mates Andy Thompson and David Delaney after scoring for Shannon v Belfast Harlequins in the AIB AIL Division One final.

BELOW Greystones celebrate after winning the AIB AIL Division Three final against Instonians.

by Belfast Harlequins and Trinity College. This final was a close affair, but two splendid tries by Bohs saw off their rivals.

In the third division final, Greystones had a well-merited win over Instonians 39-20, the winners embarking on a seven-try scoring spree. It was a fine, entertaining, open game, with Greystones having the advantage of the former senior interprovincials Colin and Shane McEntee in their back row. Greystones suffered only a single defeat during the season.

And the future? A significant success was the Grand Slam by the Irish Schools in 2005. They beat England 27-18 in Cork, Wales 33-13 in Pontypool and France 9-3 in Athlone. This means that they have now achieved the Grand Slam twice in three seasons.

Schools rugby is a major feature in the Irish game, but does it herald a major effect on the sport in this country? The U19s did poorly in the World Cup for that age group in Durban in 2005 and the bulk of the team were last season's successful schools side!

BELOW Mike Storey in the thick of it for UL Bohemians as they win the AIB AIL Division Two final against St Mary's College.

France: Biarritz Top the 16

by CHRIS THAU

'The minor miracle of the battle at the top has been the consistency of Biarritz Olympique, by far the least well-resourced and well-supported of the trio.'

T he momentous battles at both championship and relegation ends of the Top 16 league have been among the highlights of the 2004-05 French domestic season. At the top, the epic encounters between Toulouse, Paris, Biarritz and Bourgoin kept the rugby public on the edge of their seats until the very end of the season, while the fascinating clashes at the relegation end had a similar effect. Indeed the French premier league top flight underwent major surgery at the end of the season, as the Top 16 became the Top 14 for 2006. Three clubs went: the giants of the 1970s Béziers, as well as Auch and Grenoble. Meanwhile, Toulon, after five years in the 'wilderness' of the second division, returned to the elite.

This year the troika of Biarritz, Paris and Toulouse have dominated French and European rugby with authority. And with the likely re-emergence of Montferrand among the elite of French clubs, the possibility of all-French Heineken Cup semi-finals next season should not be discounted. For Stade Toulousain, the H-Cup, as the French call it (French law prohibits the advertising of alcohol), was mission accomplished, as they put Leicester to sword in the semi-final and then defeated arch-rivals Stade Français in the final at Murrayfield. It was Toulouse's emphatic reply to the crushing 40-19 defeat at the hands of the Parisians in the second half of the season.

Biarritz, meanwhile, defeated by Stade Français in the other H-Cup semi-final, had nowhere to go but back to the drawing board. While their rivals exchanged punches in an exhausting final, they had time and space to regroup, rest and plan the closing stages of the French championship campaign. That in the end may have made a difference – Biarritz were slightly fresher, more composed and perhaps more relaxed as the epic championship final drew to a close.

The championship semi-final against Toulouse offered Fabien Galthié's Stade Français the opportunity for H-Cup revenge. It is true that the two sides know each other so well and they are so finely balanced that only minor errors or moments of unquantifiable genius can make the difference. This time, the narrow defeat in the H-Cup final galvanised the Parisians to a great defensive effort, which combined with a dynamic and active attack to secure them a hard-fought 23-18 win. However, the effect of this huge clash of wills and energy was to tell against them in the final. In the other semi-final an equally finely balanced contest saw Biarritz nudge ahead of Bourgoin, thanks to a try by Nicolas Brusque in the closing stages of a match of enormous intensity and tension.

And so to the final. The story of this epic match, which ended 37-34 after extra time (31-31 after 80 minutes), cannot be written without mention of the immense efforts of the Biarritz back row of captain and Man of the Match Thomas Lievremont, Serge Betsen and Imanol Harinordoquy. Then there was the return from injury of giant lock Jérôme Thion, who had an outstanding match against his counterpart, Paris skipper David Auradou; the sensational emergence of try scorer Jean-Baptiste Gobelet, a deceptively fast wing with the build of a wing forward; and of course the contribution of Dimitri Yachvili, who scored 29 points in the final, a new French record, including the winning penalty in injury time. In the end, in a match dominated by the kicking of David Skrela, Yachvili and Biarritz fly half Julien Peyrelongue, it was the will to win and perhaps the staying power of the Biarritz men that tipped the balance. This was the seventh time Biarritz had reached the final and was their fourth title, having also won in 1935, 1939 and 2002.

The minor miracle of the battle at the top has been the consistency of Biarritz Olympique, by far the least well-resourced and well-supported of the trio. Squashed between the two giants of French rugby, Stade Toulousain and Stade Français, Biarritz seem to owe their success in the French championship more to divine justice than to sound rugby

PREVIOUS PAGE Biarritz scrum half Dimitri Yachvili escapes from Rémy Martin and Stéphane Glas during his record-breaking performance in the Top 16 final.

RIGHT Biarritz celebrate with the Top 16 trophy after winning the final 37-34.

principles. The Basques, unable to match the human and financial resources of the Parisians and Toulouse, have been making efforts to stay competitive through a combination of shrewd investment and coaching expertise. One should not exclude the 'benefactor', Serge Kampf, the charismatic owner of Cap Gemini, France's largest software manufacturer, who has poured considerable amounts into the coffers of the Basques.

The coaching duties are expertly and discreetly carried out by Patrice Lagisquet, one of the few great players to have successfully made the transition to top-level coaching, and the newly arrived Jacques Delmas. Yet they are only the tip of the iceberg. Below the water, it is the judicious investment in playing resources and the low-key management style of one of game's most astute and experienced administrators, former RWC director and IRB treasurer Marcel Martin, that really makes the difference. M Martin, the man who created the commercial framework that secured the financial success of the RWC, has launched himself into the Biarritz 'adventure' with a passion and level of competence unmatched by his counterparts. This is the secret weapon that makes Biarritz competitive well beyond their moderate means.

Wragge&Co

strength &
depth

making size and resource count on the field (and off)

At Wragge & Co, our lawyers combine their expertise to provide advice that's specific to your needs and focused on your business. With dedicated teams of experts to tackle all your legal issues, we bring strength of resource and depth of knowledge to provide practical, commercial solutions. Give us a 'try'.

Wragge & Co LLP is a Limited Liability Partnership
Birmingham London Brussels
T +44 (0)870 903 1000
mail@wragge.com
www.wragge.com

in association with
Graf von Westphalen Bappert & Modest

Italy: Calvisano Break the Jinx

by CHRIS THAU

'With veterans Massimo Ravazzolo at full back and Paolo Vaccari at centre ... Calvisano, ably led by ... Paul Griffen, showed not only great determination and courage but also some streetwise ability to stay in control and eventually win.'

After failures in four consecutive final play-offs of the Italian Super 10 national league, Ghial Calvisano managed to overcome the jinx in the fifth and defeat arch-rivals Benetton Treviso 25-20 in an epic final in Padua. This was Calvisano's first championship title in the comparatively short history of the present club, which came into being after a merger with the once famous Amatori Milano in 1998. The new club not only came into the playing assets and archives of Milano, but with former Milano president Sandro Manzoni taking over as president of the merged

entity, they also inherited the ambitions of the former champions. While the highest accolade attained by pre-merger Calvisano – formed in 1970 – was a fourth place in the league in 1997, Milano, one of Italy's oldest clubs, had won the *Scudetto* no less than 18 times, incuding once as Ambrosiana Milano in the inaugural year of 1929.

This was also a first for young coach Andrea Cavinato, in his first year in charge at Calvisano; and what a difference the former Treviso and Casale scrum half has made to the club's fortunes. Cavinato, a former coach of Italy age-group teams (he coached the U17s, U19s and U21s), prepared the team carefully to peak for the final round. In the league – disrupted by the death of Pope John Paul II – Calvisano lost six of their 18 home-and-away matches to finish third with 59 points behind Treviso and Viadana, another ambitious club in the north. In the semi-final play-offs, Calvisano managed to sneak past Viadana, winning 16-9 at home after a 13-all draw in the away match, and then surprised Treviso in the final in Padua.

With veterans Massimo Ravazzolo at full back and Paolo Vaccari at centre – the only two Calvisano-born-and-bred players in the club's cosmopolitan line-up – Calvisano, ably led by Italy's new scrum half, Dunedin-born Paul Griffen, showed not only great determination and courage but also some streetwise ability to stay in control and eventually win. They tackled like men possessed and managed to derail Treviso's well-oiled machine, with New Zealand-born fly half Gerard Fraser producing a virtuoso performance in the scoring department of an entertaining match. Fraser, in an inspired one-man show, scored all Calvisano's 25 points, with a try, one conversion and six penalties to Benetton's two tries, two conversions, one dropped goal and one penalty.

While Calvisano took the silverware, Leonessa Brescia, coached by Wales's Lynn Howells, collected the wooden spoon and descended into the second division, since the club was simply unable to match both the chequebooks and accordingly the firepower of the likes of Treviso, Viadana, Calvisano, Catania or Rovigo. Instead, the paupers of Italian rugby had to concentrate on developing talent from their own nursery, something Howells has always been very good at, as he proved during his days at Pontypridd. Such was the success of Howells in developing a new generation of talent at Leonessa that the club offered him a three-year extension to his contract, a rather unusual way to reward a coach whose team has just been relegated.

But as the Italian Super 10 was entering its final stages, an insistent rumour started circulating through Italian rugby. John Kirwan, although he had seemingly signed a contract that took him past 2007, was going to be replaced as national coach by a Frenchman, either former coach Georges Coste or, even more exciting, Pierre Berbizier, the former scrum half and coach of France. In this Latin environment, a rumour is usually a forewarning that something is about to happen. Indeed, without much ado, in his calm, understated manner, Kirwan left at the beginning of the summer. FIR president Giancarlo Dondi unveiled his new signing, Pierre Berbizier, arguably the most successful coach in French, if not European, rugby history.

Berbizier, who led France to a Five Nations Grand Slam and to a bronze medal at RWC 1995, is the only European coach to have won Test series in both South Africa and New Zealand. After three years in charge of France, he had a moderately successful stint with Narbonne in the French Top 16.

FACING PAGE Italy's new national coach, Pierre Berbizier, at a press conference in Melbourne during the 2005 tour of Argentina and Australia.

PAGE 135 Biarritz wing Jean-Baptiste Gobelet runs into Gerard Fraser and Massimo Ravazzolo as Paul Griffen looks on, during the December 2004 European Cup clash at Calvisano.

He then left French rugby in a blaze of publicity some four and a half years ago, claiming that drug abuse was rife among professional players. Under his management Italy left for a tour of Argentina and Australia. Despite losing heavily to the Wallabies, the Italians surprised the world and themselves by sharing the Test series with the Pumas.

Defeated 35-21 in the first Test in Salta, Berbizier's new charges found the energy and resources to fight back and narrowly win the second Test 30-29, after a bruising battle in Cordoba. The Italian forwards fought like dervishes, with captain Marco Bortolami eventually given his marching orders to follow an earlier yellow card. Argentinian-born fly half Ramiro Pez, unceremoniously dropped by John Kirwan for RWC 2003, re-emerged with a bang, scoring one of the three Italian tries, with Gonzalo Canale and Sergio Parisse the authors of the other two. 'At least all three were born in Argentina,' observed a stunned Argentinian journalist chewing a mouthful of sour grapes.

A Summary of the Season 2004-05

by BILL MITCHELL

INTERNATIONAL RUGBY

AUSTRALIA TO EUROPE
NOVEMBER 2004

Opponents	Results
SCOTLAND	W 31-14
FRANCE	L 14-27
SCOTLAND	W 31-17
ENGLAND	W 21-19

Played 4 Won 3 Lost 1

SOUTH AFRICA TO EUROPE & SOUTH AMERICA
NOVEMBER & DECEMBER 2004

Opponents	Results
WALES	W 38-36
IRELAND	L 12-17
ENGLAND	L 16-32
SCOTLAND	W 45-10
ARGENTINA	W 39-7

Played 5 Won 3 Lost 2

CANADA TO EUROPE
NOVEMBER 2004

Opponents	Results
ITALY	L 6-51
ENGLAND	L 0-70

Played 2 Lost 2

JAPAN TO EUROPE
NOVEMBER 2004

Opponents	Results
SCOTLAND	L 8-100
WALES	L 0-98

Played 2 Lost 2

NEW ZEALAND TO EUROPE
NOVEMBER 2004

Opponents	Results
ITALY	W 59-10
WALES	W 26-25
FRANCE	W 45-6
Barbarians	W 47-19

Played 4 Won 4

ARGENTINA TO EUROPE
NOVEMBER 2004

Opponents	Results
FRANCE	W 24-14
IRELAND	L 19-21

Played 2 Won 1 Lost 1

UNITED STATES TO EUROPE
NOVEMBER 2004

Opponents	Results
IRELAND	L 6-55
ITALY	L 25-43

Played 2 Lost 2

BRITISH & IRISH LIONS TO NEW ZEALAND
JUNE & JULY 2005

Opponents	Results
ARGENTINA	D 25-25
(played in Cardiff on 23 May)	
Bay of Plenty	W 34-20
Taranaki	W 36-19
New Zealand Maori	L 13-19
Wellington	W 23-6
Otago	W 30-19
Southland	W 26-16
NEW ZEALAND	L 3-21
Manawatu	W 109-6
NEW ZEALAND	L 8-48
Auckland	W 17-13
NEW ZEALAND	L 19-38

Played 12 Won 7 Drawn 1 Lost 4

WALES TO NORTH AMERICA
JUNE 2005

Opponents	Results
UNITED STATES	W 77-3
CANADA	W 60-3

Played 2 Won 2

ITALY TO ARGENTINA AND AUSTRALIA
JUNE 2005

Opponents	Results
ARGENTINA	L 21-35
ARGENTINA	W 30-29
AUSTRALIA	L 21-69

Played 3 Won 1 Lost 2

IRELAND TO JAPAN
JUNE 2005

Opponents	Results
JAPAN	W 44-12
JAPAN	W 47-18

Played 2 Won 2

FRANCE TO SOUTH AFRICA AND AUSTRALIA
JUNE 2005

Opponents	Results
SOUTH AFRICA	D 30-30
SOUTH AFRICA	L 13-27
AUSTRALIA	L 31-37

Played 3 Drawn 1 Lost 2

ROYAL BANK OF SCOTLAND SIX NATIONS
CHAMPIONSHIP 2005

Results

France	16	Scotland	9
Wales	11	England	9
Italy	17	Ireland	28
Italy	8	Wales	38
Scotland	13	Ireland	40
England	17	France	18
Scotland	18	Italy	10
France	18	Wales	24
Ireland	19	England	13
Ireland	19	France	26
England	39	Italy	7
Scotland	22	Wales	46
Italy	13	France	56
Wales	32	Ireland	20
England	43	Scotland	22

	P	W	D	L	F	A	Pts
Wales	5	5	0	0	151	77	10
France	5	4	0	1	134	82	8
Ireland	5	3	0	2	126	101	6
England	5	2	0	3	121	77	4
Scotland	5	1	0	4	84	155	2
Italy	5	0	0	5	55	179	0

IRB SUPER CUP 2005

Semi-finals

Canada	30	United States	26
Japan	23	Romania	16

Third-place Play-off

Romania	22	United States	28

Final

Japan	10	Canada	15

CHURCHILL CUP 2005

Semi-finals

United States	30	Argentina	34
Canada	5	England	29

Third-place Play-off

Canada	19	United States	20

Final

Argentina	16	England	45

NELSON MANDELA TROPHY

Australia	30	South Africa	12
South Africa	33	Australia	20

(Australia win 50-45 on aggregate)

IRB 'REBUILDING AFTER THE TSUNAMI'
RUGBY AID MATCH

North	19	South	54

OTHER INTERNATIONAL MATCHES

Argentina	68	Japan	36
Wales	66	Romania	7
Romania	19	Scotland	39
New Zealand	91	Fiji	0
Australia	74	Samoa	7
South Africa	134	Uruguay	3

INTERNATIONAL BENEFIT MATCH

Martin Johnson XV	33	Jonah Lomu XV	29

SIX NATIONS UNDER 21 CHAMPIONSHIP 2005

Results

France	12	Scotland	8
Wales	32	England	21
Italy	21	Ireland	33
Italy	3	Wales	40
Scotland	16	Ireland	8
England	17	France	29
Scotland	38	Italy	12
Ireland	6	England	28
France	19	Wales	20
Scotland	7	Wales	31
Ireland	13	France	20
England	31	Italy	14
Italy	0	France	51
Wales	32	Ireland	5
England	17	Scotland	19

	P	W	D	L	F	A	Pts
Wales	5	5	0	0	155	55	10
France	5	4	0	1	122	58	8
Scotland	5	3	0	2	88	80	6
England	5	2	0	3	114	91	4
Ireland	5	1	0	4	65	117	2
Italy	5	0	0	5	50	193	0

a new breed of blackjack

Blackjack, the latest title in our range of instant, non-download spread betting games, has some neat twists. Don't like the hand you're dealt? Then bust it and deal the next one - you don't have to bet until you've got the hand you like. Which other game also lets you switch allegiance and bet on the dealer winning? Visit sportingindex.com and bet for real or just play for fun.

Sports spread betting involves a high level of risk and you can lose more than your original stake. It is not suitable for everyone so please ensure you understand the risks involved and only bet with money you can afford to lose. Sporting Index is authorised and regulated by the Financial Services Authority.

sportingindex.com   08000 96 96 45   ch4 text p604   press red on sky

Sporting Index
World Leaders in Sports Spread Betting

UNDER 21 WORLD CHAMPIONSHIP 2005

(Held in June in Argentina)

Eleventh-place Play-off
Canada 33 Italy 30

Ninth-place Play-off
Ireland 34 Samoa 17

Seventh-place Play-off
England 57 Wales 32

Fifth-place Play-off
Argentina 39 Scotland 7

Semi-finals
France 16 Australia 28
South Africa 16 New Zealand 12

Third-place Play-off
New Zealand 47 France 21

Final
South Africa 24 Australia 20

UNDER 19 WORLD CHAMPIONSHIP 2005

(Held in April in South Africa)

Eleventh-place Play-off
Japan 24 Georgia 0

Ninth-place Play-off
Ireland 15 Scotland 8

Seventh-place Play-off
Argentina 13 Romania 21

Fifth-place Play-off
Wales 10 France 13

Semi-finals
New Zealand 25 Australia 25
(New Zealand win 4-3 on penalties)
South Africa 17 England 12

Third-place Play-off
England 21 Australia 29

Final
South Africa 20 New Zealand 15

WOMEN'S SIX NATIONS CHAMPIONSHIP 2005

Results

France	22	Scotland	15
Wales	0	England	81
Spain	19	Ireland	17
Spain	10	Wales	10
Scotland	15	Ireland	5
England	10	France	13
France	48	Wales	0
Ireland	0	England	32
Scotland	19	Spain	3
England	76	Spain	0
Ireland	0	France	34
Scotland	22	Wales	5
Wales	6	Ireland	11
England	22	Scotland	10
Spain	0	France	39

	P	W	D	L	F	A	Pts
France	5	5	0	0	156	25	10
England	5	4	0	1	221	23	8
Scotland	5	3	0	2	81	57	6
Spain	5	1	1	3	32	161	3
Ireland	5	1	0	4	33	106	2
Wales	5	0	1	4	21	172	1

IRB SEVENS SERIES FINALS 2004-05

Dubai
England 26 Fiji 21

South Africa (George)
New Zealand 33 Fiji 19

New Zealand (Wellington)
Argentina 7 New Zealand 31

United States (Los Angeles)
Argentina 5 New Zealand 34

Singapore
New Zealand 26 England 5

England (Twickenham)
South Africa 21 England 12

France (Paris)
France 28 Fiji 19

New Zealand win the IRB World Sevens Series; 2nd: Fiji; 3rd: England

RWC SEVENS 2005

(Held in March in Hong Kong)

Final
Fiji 29 New Zealand 19

TRI-NATIONS 2005

South Africa	22	Australia	16
South Africa	22	New Zealand	16
Australia	13	New Zealand	30
Australia	19	South Africa	22
New Zealand	31	South Africa	27
New Zealand	34	Australia	24

New Zealand are the 2005 Tri-nations champions

Rugby crazy?

We're mad about it too!

That's why we're the official energy partner to England Rugby and sponsor of the Powergen Cup.

But our support doesn't stop there. Our National Rugby Community Programme is the largest of its kind in the world reaching over 400,000 people each season.

From the champions of today to the champions of tomorrow, we're giving everyone the chance to go rugby crazy!

powergen.co.uk

Positive Energy

CLUB, COUNTY AND DIVISIONAL RUGBY

ENGLAND

Powergen Cup
Quarter-finals

Gloucester	21	Bristol	0
Northampton	19	Leeds	24
Sale	23	Bath	24
Saracens	15	London Irish	21

Semi-finals

Gloucester	19	Bath	24
	(after extra time)		
Leeds	15	London Irish	6

Final

Leeds	20	Bath	12

Zurich Premiership

	P	W	D	L	F	A	BP	Pts
Leicester	22	15	3	4	665	323	12	78
Wasps	22	15	1	6	561	442	11	73
Sale	22	13	0	9	513	442	8	60
Bath	22	12	2	8	407	366	6	58
Saracens	22	12	2	8	384	428	5	57
Gloucester	22	10	1	11	407	487	5	47
Newcastle	22	9	2	11	475	596	7	47
Leeds	22	9	0	13	380	431	7	43
Worcester	22	9	0	13	365	493	6	42
London Irish	22	8	0	14	378	421	8	40
Northampton	22	8	0	14	410	473	8	40
Harlequins	22	6	1	15	416	459	12	38

Zurich Premiership Play-offs
Semi-final

Wasps	43	Sale	22

Final

Leicester	14	Wasps	39

Wildcard Play-offs
Semi-finals

Gloucester	23	Newcastle	16
Saracens	43	Sale	22

Final

Saracens	24	Gloucester	16

National Leagues
1st Division Champions: Bristol
Runners-up: Exeter
2nd Division Champions: Doncaster
Runners-up: Newbury
3rd Division North Champions: Halifax
Runners-up: Macclesfield
3rd Division South Champions: Barking
Runners-up: Redruth

Powergen Challenge Shield Final

Bedford	14	Plymouth Albion	13

Powergen Intermediate Cup Final

Morley	21	Westoe	11

Powergen Junior Vase Final

Sheffield Tigers	30	Solihull	13

County Championship Final

Devon	22	Lancashire	16

County Shield Final

North Midlands	13	Hertfordshire	20

University Match

Oxford U	18	Cambridge U	11

University Second Teams Match

CU LX Club	18	OU Greyhounds	22

University U21 Match

Oxford U U21	17	Cambridge U U21	20

Other University Matches

Oxford U Whippets	18	Cambridge U U21A	8
Oxford U Colleges	15	Cambridge U Colls	12

Women's University Match

Cambridge U	0	Oxford U	20

Women's University Second Teams Match

Oxford U	5	Cambridge U	10

British Universities Sports Association
Men's Winners: Loughborough University
Women's Winners: Loughborough University

Hospitals Cup Winners: Imperial Medicals
Inter-Services Champions: The Army

Middlesex Sevens Winners: The Army

Rosslyn Park National Schools Sevens (sponsored by Wooden Spoon)
Festival Winners: Wellington College
Colts Winners: Sedbergh School
Junior Winners: Cwm Rhyni
Preparatory Schools Winners: Sedbergh School
Girls Schools Winners: Rickmansworth School
Open Winners: Millfield School

Daily Mail Schools Day (at Twickenham)
Under 18 Cup Winners: Exeter College
Under 18 Vase Winners: Crossley Heath
Under 15 Cup Winners: St Benedict's, Ealing
Under 15 Vase Winners: Maidstone GS

RFUW Rugby World National Cup Final

Wasps	20	Saracens	13

National Cup Title Match

Leodiensians	10	Carlisle	5

Under 17 National Cup

Worcester	18	Chester	10

National Challenge Cup

Olney	15	London Welsh	0

NEXT

ARE PROUD TO SUPPORT

WOODEN SPOON RUGBY WORLD '06

SCOTLAND

BT Cup Final
Boroughmuir   39   Dundee HSFP   25
BT Shield Final
Murrayfield Wdrs   25   Livingston   13
BT Bowl Final
Ardrossan Acads   28   Greenock Wdrs   11

Scottish Sevens Winners
Selkirk: Newcastle Falcons
Kelso: Jed-Forest
Gala: Watsonians
Melrose: Stellenbosch University
Hawick: Newcastle Falcons
Berwick: Jed-Forest
Langholm: Newcastle Falcons
Peebles: Watsonians
Earlston: Watsonians
Jed-Forest: Melrose
Kings of Sevens title: Melrose

BT Scotland Premiership
Division One

	P	W	D	L	F	A	BP	Pts
Glasgow Hawks	22	20	0	2	770	357	17	97
Heriots RC	22	15	1	6	623	417	14	76
Boroughmuir	22	14	0	8	595	421	14	70
Melrose	22	12	1	9	595	587	11	61
Biggar	22	11	1	10	441	451	10	56
Aberdeen GSFP	22	11	0	11	545	460	11	55
Hawick	22	10	1	11	469	611	7	49
Ayr	22	10	1	11	489	500	6	48
Watsonians	22	9	2	11	526	588	8	48
Currie	22	8	1	13	492	537	10	44
Glasgow HA	22	7	0	15	458	556	11	39
Gala	22	1	0	21	312	840	8	12

Champions: Glasgow Hawks
Relegated: Glasgow HA, Gala

Division Two

	P	W	D	L	F	A	BP	Pts
Stirling County	22	21	0	1	490	270	18	102
Stewart's M'ville	22	16	2	4	583	365	13	81
Jed-Forest	22	16	0	6	480	342	4	68
Dundee HSFP	22	12	0	10	530	415	12	60
Haddington	22	17	1	9	435	338	10	56
Edinburgh Acads	22	11	0	11	404	462	7	51
Berwick	22	11	0	11	426	497	6	50
Kelso	22	9	0	13	354	483	7	43
Selkirk	22	9	0	13	400	554	6	42
M'field Wdrs	22	6	0	16	379	623	10	34
Peebles	22	5	1	16	379	499	9	31
Kirkcaldy	22	1	2	19	282	630	8	16

Promoted: Stirling County (Champions), Stewart's Melville FP
Relegated: Peebles, Kirkcaldy

Division Three
Promoted: Cartha Queen's Park,
Hillhead/Jordanhill
Relegated: Preston Lodge FP, Grangemouth

WALES

Konica Minolta Cup
Quarter-finals
Aberavon   18   Newport   17
Banwen   17   Pontypridd   41
Beddau   15   Bridgend   24
Llanelli   21   Carmarthen Quins   8
Semi-finals
Aberavon   13   Pontypridd   33
Bridgend   10   Llanelli   20
Final
Llanelli   25   Pontypridd   24

Welsh Premier Division

	P	W	D	L	F	A	Pts
Neath	32	27	0	5	1208	401	81
Newport	32	25	0	7	905	526	72
Bridgend	32	23	0	9	736	475	66
Llanelli	32	20	0	12	784	587	60
Aberavon	32	19	0	13	782	761	57
Cross Keys	32	19	0	13	668	752	57
Carmarthen	32	18	1	13	785	579	55
Cardiff	32	18	0	14	835	662	54
Swansea	32	17	2	13	837	728	53
Pontypridd	32	17	1	14	729	610	52
Ebbw Vale	32	14	0	18	644	819	39
Pontypool	32	12	1	19	635	786	37
Bedwas	32	12	0	20	560	747	36
Llandovery	32	12	0	20	597	873	36
Caerphilly	32	8	0	24	695	945	24
Llanharan	32	4	1	27	548	1054	13
Newbridge	32	4	0	28	540	1183	9

Relegated: Caerphilly, Llanharan, Newbridge

Lloyds TSB Welsh Leagues
Division One

	P	W	D	L	F	A	Pts
Maesteg	28	24	2	2	881	344	74
Glamorgan Wdrs	28	23	0	5	751	302	69
Beddau	28	19	1	8	759	446	58
Whitland	28	18	1	9	551	313	55
Bonymaen	28	17	0	11	678	476	51
Llangennech	28	15	2	11	595	540	47
UWIC	28	13	2	13	746	573	41
Narberth	28	13	2	13	640	595	41
Blackwood	28	12	1	15	456	511	37
Builth Wells	28	12	0	16	487	521	36
Fleur de Lys	28	11	1	16	535	653	34
Bridgend Athletic	28	10	1	17	525	724	31
Carmarthen Ath	28	10	1	17	529	558	31
Tonmawr	28	6	0	48	404	619	18
Brynmawr	28	0	0	28	174	1535	–6*

* Denotes six points deducted

Promoted: Maesteg, Glamorgan Wanderers
Relegated: Bridgend Athletic, Carmarthen Athletic, Tonmawr, Brynmawr

Division Two East Champions: Ystrad Rhondda
Runners-up: Merthyr
Division Two West Champions: Cwmllynwell
Runners-up: Waunarlwydd

IRELAND

AIB League
Division One

	P	W	D	L	F	A	BP	Pts
Shannon	13	11	0	2	395	195	7	51
Garryowen	13	11	0	2	286	196	4	48
Belfast H'quins	13	10	0	3	309	148	6	46
Clontarf	13	8	0	5	225	197	6	38
Ballymena	13	8	0	5	338	234	8	36
Univ Coll Dublin	13	7	1	5	275	238	4	34
Dungannon	13	6	1	6	212	270	2	28
Cork Constitution	13	5	1	7	233	247	5	27
Galwegians	13	4	1	8	236	333	5	23
Blackrock College	13	3	2	8	209	248	6	22
Buccaneers	13	5	0	8	196	358	1	21
Dublin University	13	1	5	7	207	246	6	20
County Carlow	13	4	0	9	210	329	3	19
Lansdowne	13	3	1	9	175	267	4	18

No relegation owing to league enlargement

AIB League Play-offs
Semi-finals

Garryowen	15	Belfast Harlequins	18
Shannon	21	Clontarf	11

Final

Shannon	25	Belfast Harlequins	20

Division One Play-off

Lansdowne	29	Univ Coll Cork	6

Division Two
Champions: UL Bohemians
Runners-up: St Mary's College

Division Three
Champions: Greystones
Runners-up: Instonians

Senior Cup Winners
Munster: Shannon
Leinster: St Mary's College
Ulster: Ballymena
Connacht: Galwegians

Senior League Winners
Munster: Shannon
Leinster: Naas
Ulster: Ballymena and Belfast Harlequins (shared)
Connacht: Galwegians

CELTIC CUP

Semi-finals

Leinster	17	Munster	23
Scarlets	23	Ospreys	15

Final

Munster	27	Scarlets	16

CELTIC LEAGUE

	P	W	D	L	F	A	BP	Pts
Ospreys	20	14	1	3	508	267	10	76
Munster	20	15	1	5	470	331	7	69
Leinster	20	12	1	7	425	327	7	53
Scarlets	20	9	0	11	452	429	10	50
Dragons	20	11	0	9	381	436	5	45
Glasgow	20	8	1	11	465	466	11	45
Edinburgh	20	9	0	11	409	407	8	44
Ulster	20	9	0	11	363	387	7	43
Blues	20	8	1	11	350	404	6	40
Connacht	20	7	1	12	317	407	7	37
Borders	20	3	0	17	337	556	6	14

FRANCE

'Top 16'

	P	W	D	L	F	A	BP	Pts
Stade Français	30	21	2	7	858	613	12	100
Biarritz	30	20	0	10	838	488	16	96
Bourgoin	30	20	2	8	855	648	12	96
Toulouse	30	19	0	11	875	574	18	94
Perpignan	30	18	1	11	688	583	12	86
Castres	30	17	3	10	704	678	10	74
Agen	30	16	1	13	674	568	11	77
Clermont	30	16	2	12	745	647	9	77
Brive	30	14	1	15	668	745	8	66
Narbonne	30	13	2	15	588	755	7	63
Montpellier	30	12	0	18	628	765	13	61
Bayonne	30	12	3	15	587	763	6	60
Pau	30	10	2	18	605	715	11	55
Grenoble	30	7	2	21	580	842	10	42
Béziers	30	6	3	21	600	876	8	38
Auch	30	7	0	23	503	736	9	37

Semi-finals

Stade Français	23	Toulouse	18
Biarritz	32	Bourgoin	27

Final

Stade Français	34	Biarritz	37

ITALY

'Super 10'

Final

Calvisano	25	Benetton Treviso	20

NEW ZEALAND

National Provincial Championship 2004

Final

Wellington	27	Canterbury	40

Ranfurly Shield holders: Canterbury

SOUTH AFRICA

Currie Cup 2004

Final
Blue Bulls	42	Cheetahs	33

BARBARIANS

Opponents	Results
PORTUGAL	W 66-34
Combined Services	L 36-38
NEW ZEALAND	L 19-47
East Midlands	W 48-17
Leicester	L 19-42
SCOTLAND	L 7-38
ENGLAND	W 52-39

Played 7 Won 3 Lost 4

SUPER 12 TOURNAMENT 2005

	P	W	D	L	F	A	BP	Pts
Crusaders	11	9	0	2	459	281	8	44
Waratahs	11	9	0	2	322	174	8	44
Bulls	11	7	0	4	301	229	6	34
Hurricanes	11	8	0	3	283	248	2	34
Brumbies	11	5	1	5	260	268	7	29
Chiefs	11	5	1	5	272	250	6	28
Blues	11	6	0	5	243	216	3	27
Highlanders	11	6	1	4	221	214	1	27
Stormers	11	3	1	7	215	320	4	18
Reds	11	3	0	8	185	282	5	17
Cats	11	1	1	9	226	326	7	13
Sharks	11	1	1	9	205	384	5	11

Semi-finals
Crusaders	47	Hurricanes	7
Waratahs	23	Bulls	13

Final
Crusaders	35	Waratahs	25

HEINEKEN CUP 2005

Quarter-finals
Biarritz	19	Munster	10
Leinster	13	Leicester	29
Stade Français	48	Newcastle	8
Toulouse	37	Northampton	9

Semi-finals
Leicester	19	Toulouse	27
Stade Français	20	Biarritz	17

Final
Toulouse	18	Stade Français	12

(after extra time – 12-12 after 80 minutes)

EUROPEAN CHALLENGE CUP 2005

Semi-finals
Connacht	18	Sale Sharks	25
Sale Sharks	59	Connacht	9

(aggregate 84-27)

Pau	37	Brive	16
Brive	27	Pau	13

(aggregate 50-43)

Final
Pau	3	Sale Sharks	27

EUROPEAN SHIELD 2005

Final
Auch	23	Worcester	10

AFTER ALL THAT
THINKING YOU DESERVE A REST

DECISIONS, DECISIONS

CALIFORNIA?
THE CARIBBEAN? CHILE?

delta.com/uk

Delta offers daily non-stop flights from London and Manchester to the U.S., with convenient connections to over 170 destinations throughout the U.S., Latin America and the Caribbean.

For further information please call 0800 414 767 or visit our website.

PREVIEW OF THE
SEASON 2005-06

Key Players 2005-06

by IAN ROBERTSON

ENGLAND

MARK CUETO

Having scored a try on his 2001 debut for Sale Sharks, Mark Cueto was selected to tour Argentina with England the same year and also represented England at sevens, aged just 21. Cueto's combination of power, pace and killer instinct with the try line in sight soon made him one of the most prolific scorers in the game.

Cueto marked his international debut against Canada in November 2004 with a brace of tries and added another each against South Africa and Australia to give him four tries in his first three Tests. As the form wing and one of Europe's most deadly finishers last season, it was not surprising to see him end up top try scorer in the Six Nations. With a strike rate of eight tries in eight matches for his country, he is likely to be a fixture in England's squad for years to come.

Extremely unlucky to have been overlooked by Sir Clive Woodward in his original Lions selection, Cueto was a late inclusion in the 45-man touring party when he was called up as a replacement for the injured Iain Balshaw.

MARTIN CORRY

A Test debut against Argentina in 1997 proved to be something of a false dawn for Martin Corry, as Clive Woodward settled on a starting back row of Dallaglio, Hill and Back that became entrenched until the World Cup victory in 2003. Even after breaking into the Lions Test team in Australia in 2001, Corry remained virtually redundant during England's march to global glory.

Everything changed last season. Corry was an inspiration for the Tigers, was outstanding in the autumn victory over South Africa and put in some fantastic performances during the Six Nations. He was appointed stand-in national captain when Jason Robinson suffered an injury, led the Lions against NZ Maori and was named vice-captain for the first Test in Christchurch. Corry is a player's player. He is committed, abrasive when necessary, a powerful ball carrier, defensively sound and a useful line-out option – but he goes about his work in an unfussy manner. Given the intense competition for places in the back row, it is a tribute to his resilience and persistence that he has already accumulated 37 England caps.

SCOTLAND

GORDON ROSS

To call Gordon Ross's international career a stop-start affair would be an understatement. His Test debut in 2001 couldn't have gone much better, as he scored a Murrayfield record 23 points against Tonga to earn the Man of the Match award. The future seemed bright but, remarkably, he was dropped – the first of six such personal setbacks at the hands of the Scottish selectors. It took him fully 12 months to fight his way back into favour, and after returning against Romania he orchestrated the sensational 21-6 victory over South Africa at Murrayfield. Yet once again Ross's sense of satisfaction was short-lived, as coach Ian McGeechan reinstated Gregor Townsend against Fiji. And so the process went on. He played in two World Cup warm-up matches, but after being selected for the tournament opener against Japan, he failed to resurface.

Ross returned to impress in the 2004 win over Samoa but was then dropped by Matt Williams in favour of Dan Parks. Then during last season's Six Nations, Ross came on against Wales and helped his side back from the brink of humiliation, earning himself a full 80 minutes against England. With a greater running capability now allied to his kicking nous and improved impact in the tackle, Ross's international prospects are looking up.

GORDON BULLOCH

Gordon Bulloch is Scotland's most-capped hooker, having played 75 times since his debut eight years ago, an indication of his resilience and durability. Not only one of the most experienced players in Scottish rugby, he is also recognised as being one of the hardest. Respected throughout the world for his total commitment and competitive nature, the 30-year-old is a natural-born leader who has captained his country on nine occasions.

Bulloch has proven himself at the highest level, playing in two World Cups and winning a cap on the 2001 Lions tour to Australia. His robust, steely attitude, combined with a tremendous work ethic, led to him being named as one of only three Scots in the 2005 Lions squad. He is always dependable, and his hard-nosed, gritty approach won enormous respect from his British and Irish team-mates when he captained the Lions against Manawatu.

Bulloch enjoyed a career-spanning ten years with Glasgow, during which time he played 138 games for the club in its current format, plus 29 appearances for the district in the early years of professional rugby. It will be extremely hard for him to detach himself from his home city and end an association with the club that stretches back to the amateur days, but Bulloch is looking forward to a new challenge in 2005-06 having signed for Leeds Tykes.

WALES

STEPHEN JONES

The former Llanelli stand-off has flourished since he left Wales for a fresh start in French rugby. Jones was always a dependable performer – a solid kicker, a shrewd tactician. Yet his game lacked that special spark of creativity and he was frequently content to play a percentage game. Not any more. By his own admission, training and playing in France has been an eye-opening experience, making him bolder and more instinctive. He has become better at breaking a defensive line with aggressive running and clinical passing at close quarters. Wales reaped the rewards during last season's Grand Slam campaign. Jones did the simple things as well as ever, but added a dash of flair into the bargain. He has 441 points and 48 caps to his name, and younger players, such as former club colleague Dwayne Peel, drew on Jones's international experience, helping them to grow in confidence and stature. Peel and Jones forged an impressive half-back partnership and played a major part in the crucial, backs-to-the-wall victory over France in Paris. With Clermont Auvergne, Jones finished as the Top 16's second-highest points scorer with 317. He was named in the 2005 British and Irish Lions squad and played in the first Test against the All Blacks, shifting the more high-profile fly half Jonny Wilkinson to inside centre.

MICHAEL OWEN

The responsibility of leadership inspires some players and it had just that effect on Michael Owen last season. Having started the Six Nations as someone still regarded as a promising prospect, he ended it as the 24-year-old captain who guided Wales to their first Grand Slam for 27 years. When Gareth Thomas was injured in Paris, Mike Ruddock asked Owen to take over as skipper. What followed was a monumental Welsh fightback to victory. Owen made the grade in club rugby at Pontypridd, before switching to the Newport Gwent Dragons in 2003. By that time, he had already made his Wales debut, becoming the country's 1000th international when he played against South Africa.

For a while, Owen's versatility counted against him. He was shunted between lock and the back row, failed to secure a regular starting place and missed out on selection for the 2003 World Cup. But under Ruddock he has been firmly in favour, in his preferred position of No. 8. Owen is a prototype modern loose forward – an accomplished ball player with good awareness and deft footwork. One man he impressed was Sir Clive Woodward, who not only selected him in the touring party for New Zealand but also made him captain against Argentina in Cardiff and then for the pre-first Test clash with Southland.

IRELAND

GORDON D'ARCY

Back in the early spring of 2004, Irish rugby was cock-a-hoop at the sight of two remarkably similar centres cutting a swathe through the best defences in Europe. One of the pair – Brian O'Driscoll – was a well-known commodity. But his midfield partner, one Gordon D'Arcy, had barely registered on the radar before, certainly not in international terms. So there was an almighty fuss when the younger man set that season's Six Nations alight with the sort of explosive running that his superstar sidekick was renowned for the world over. D'Arcy was strong, he was elusive and his solid frame and low centre of gravity made him difficult to bring down. His breathtaking contribution to Ireland's Triple Crown success was capped on a sunny, two-try afternoon at Lansdowne Road, when he had Scotland chasing shadows. He was named player of the tournament and subsequently nominated for the IRB's player of the year award. At the turn of the year D'Arcy was regarded as the clear favourite for the Lions Test No. 12 place, only for injury to intervene. He lasted barely half an hour of the last Six Nations before limping out of the game against Italy with a hamstring problem. The rehabilitation dragged on slowly, but he finally returned for Leinster in April, just in time to make the cut for the Lions squad.

PAUL O'CONNELL

Ever since his try-scoring international debut against Wales at the start of the 2002 Six Nations, this formidable forward has been building a reputation as Ireland's answer to Martin Johnson. England's World Cup-winning captain was a one-off, but O'Connell is certainly cut from the same cloth. He is an effective ball carrier, a supreme front-of-the-line jumper and a tough customer. O'Connell won widespread acclaim for his exploits at the 2003 World Cup. His star continued to rise, so much so that when Brian O'Driscoll was injured prior to the 2004 Six Nations, he deputised as Ireland captain; he was given the job again on a temporary basis during last season's championship. When speculation about Lions selection began towards the end of 2004, O'Connell was seen as a certainty for the Test team and even as a possible captain of the touring party.

Then, all of a sudden, his game went off the boil. As Munster battled to clinch their Heineken Cup holy grail, he was not such a commanding presence. As Ireland's Triple Crown crusade floundered against Wales, O'Connell couldn't quite summon up his usual reserves of heroic defiance. However, his form returned in the final stages of the season – a well-timed revival that carried him into the Lions squad and, ultimately, into the Test team against the All Blacks. He can be relied upon to inspire the Irish again next season.

FRANCE

DIMITRI YACHVILI

After a fine display of form in last season's Six Nations, Dimitri Yachvili has finally established himself as France's number one scrum half, having fought off competition from Jean-Baptiste Elissalde of Toulouse. A dangerous sniper at the base of the scrum, he is just as likely to dart through a gap on a solo run as he is to unleash his dangerous French back line. He is equally adept at sparking a French attack with a chip over the opposition defence and more than capable of punishing the opposition with his deadly goal-kicking boot. Yachvili was the man responsible for inflicting a 17-18 defeat on England during last season's Six Nations after slotting six penalties to accrue all of France's points. He finished the tournament as the second most accurate kicker with a 75 per cent success rate and was also the fourth highest points scorer in last season's Heineken Cup.

Yachvili is not the only member of his family to have played international rugby. He is the son of former French hooker Michel Yachvili, and his elder brother Gregoire plays for Georgia. Yachvili is the latest in a line of scrum-half 'generals' to be handed the captaincy of France, having been named by Bernard Laporte to lead the side on their 2005 summer tour of South Africa.

SEBASTIEN CHABAL

One of the most inspirational signings of 2004, Chabal took the Zurich Premiership by storm with his bulldozing runs and bone-crunching tackles. Chabal's eye-catching form in the Premiership earned him a recall to the French national side to play Scotland and England in the 2005 Six Nations. Since following his former Bourgoin boss, Philippe Saint-André, to Edgeley Park, he has repaid tenfold the faith that the current Sale Sharks coach showed in him. Having won the last of his 20 international caps to that point against the All Blacks back in the 2003 World Cup, some suggest he has the former French flyer to thank for resurrecting a flagging international career.

There certainly hasn't been any sign of flagging when on the pitch for Sale. He has been such an inspiration to the club that he was presented with the Sharks' 2005 Player of the Year award and he also pushed Martin Corry close in the race to be named the overall Zurich Player of the Season. At 6ft 3ins and 17 stones, Chabal displays primeval instincts when it comes to his attacking nature and ferocious hits. He possesses a remarkable reach and many a player has found himself enveloped in his grasp before being turned and dispossessed. He is also a world-class ball carrier and is likely to pick up more awards this season.

ITALY

MIRCO BERGAMASCO

Still living somewhat in the shadow of his elder brother Mauro, Mirco Bergamasco is starting to make a name for himself at Stade Français after the two transferred to Paris following the 2003 World Cup. After coming off the bench to face France on his international debut, Bergamasco has earned a further 22 caps in a variety of positions in the Italian back line. Traditionally lining up on the wing or at full back, he is also comfortable at centre and such versatility has made him a valuable asset to the Azzurri squad. Although Bergamasco has started to add some bulk to his previously slender frame, his game does not possess the same physicality as that of his back-row sibling, but what he lacks in brute strength, he makes up for in searing pace, which enables him to slice through the opposition defence.

Whereas Bergamasco major opted to play for Treviso, Mirco remained in his home town of Padova (Padua). Since he signed for Stade Français his game has benefited dramatically from his being surrounded by players of the highest calibre. Although he has yet to become a permanent fixture in the Stade Français starting line-up, his technical skills have noticeably improved, as has his general reading of the game. As his confidence grows he is likely to flourish on the international scene.

MARTIN LEANDRO CASTROGIOVANNI

Now 24, Martin Leandro Castrogiovanni was one of the many youngsters John Kirwan placed under the international spotlight during Italy's tour to New Zealand in the summer of 2002. He had represented the U21 side the previous year, and Castrogiovanni's induction into senior international rugby now came in the harshest possible environment, with a debut in Italy's 64-10 defeat by the All Blacks in Hamilton. He went on to make the starting line-up for the Azzurri in each of their three World Cup games in 2003, where his performances inspired the respect of team-mates and opposition alike. His reputation as one of the most promising talents on the Italian rugby horizon was cemented by his outstanding performance in Italy's 20-14 win over Scotland at the Stadio Flaminio in 2004, in which he picked up the Man of the Match award.

A fearsome tackler and a menace in the scrum, he is a front-row forward who encapsulates all the physical attributes associated with an Italian pack. Castrogiovanni is just as dangerous in the loose as he is in set play and has an impressive try-scoring record with five in twenty-seven appearances for Italy. This includes a remarkable hat-trick against Japan in July 2004 in which match he skippered the side to a 32-19 victory. Guaranteed to make a real impact again for Italy this season.

Fixtures 2005-06

AUGUST 2005

Sat, 27th — Scottish Premiership 1-3 (1)

SEPTEMBER 2005

Fri, 2nd/ Sun, 4th — Celtic League (1)

Sat, 3rd
- English Lges National 1-3 (1)
- English Senior Cup Prelim Rd
- English Junior Vase Prelim Rd
- English Lges (12s) (1)
- Welsh Lges Prem, 1 (1)
- Welsh Lges all Divs 2+3 (1)
- Scottish Premiership 1-3 (2)
- Scottish Nat Lges 1-4 (1)

Fri, 9th/ Sun, 11th — Celtic League (2)

Sat, 10th
- English Lges National 1-3 (2)
- English Lges (12s) (2)
- English Lges (10s) (1)
- Welsh Lges Prem, 1 (2)
- Welsh Lges all Divs 2+3 (2)
- Scottish Premiership 1-3 (3)
- Scottish Nat Lges 1-4 (2)

Tue, 13th — Ospreys v Dragons (Celtic Lge)
Wed, 14th — Blues v Scarlets (Celtic Lge)
Fri, 16th/ Sun, 18th — Celtic League (3)

Sat, 17th
- English Lges National 1,2 (3)
- English Senior Cup Rd 1
- English Intermediate Cup and Junior Vase Rd 1
- Welsh Lges Prem, 1 (3)
- Welsh Lges all Divs 2+3 (3)
- Scottish Premiership 1-3 (4)
- Scottish Nat Lges 1-4 (3)

Fri, 23rd/ Sun, 25th — Celtic League (4)

Sat, 24th
- English Lges National 1,2 (4)
- English Lges National 3 (3)
- English Lges (12s) (3)
- English Lges (10s) (2)
- Welsh Lges Prem, 1 (4)
- Welsh Lges all Divs 2+3 (4)
- Scottish Premiership 1-3 (5)
- Scottish Nat Lges 1-4 (4)

OCTOBER 2005

Fri, 30th Sept/ Sun, 2nd — Celtic League (5)

Sat, 1st
- English Lges National 1 (5)
- English Senior Cup Rd 2
- English Lges (12s) (4)
- English Lges (10s) (3)
- Welsh Lges Prem, 1 (5)
- Welsh Lges all Divs 2+3 (5)
- Scottish Premiership 1-3 (6)
- Scottish Nat Lges 1-4 (5)

Sat, 8th
- English Lges National 1 (6)
- English Lges National 2 (5)
- English Lges National 3 (4)
- English Lges (12s) (5)
- English Lges (10s) (4)
- Welsh Lges Prem, 1 (6)
- Welsh Lges all Divs 2+3 (6)
- Scottish Premiership 1-3 (7)

Fri, 14th/ Sun, 16th — Celtic League (6)

Sat, 15th
- English Senior Cup Rd 3
- English Intermediate Cup and Junior Vase Rd 2
- Welsh Lges Prem, 1 (7)
- Welsh Lges all Divs 2+3 (7)
- Scottish Premiership 1-3 (8)
- Scottish Nat Lges 1-4 (6)
- AIB Lges 1-3 (1)

Fri, 21st/ Sun, 23rd — European Competitions Rd 1

Sat, 22nd
- English Lges National 1 (7)
- English Lges National 2 (6)
- English Lges National 3 (5)
- English Lges (12s) (6)
- English Lges (10s) (5)
- Welsh Lges Prem, 1 (8)
- Welsh Lges all Divs 2+3 (8)
- Scottish Premiership 1-3 (9)
- Scottish Nat Lges 1-4 (7)
- AIB Lges 1-3 (2)

Sun, 23rd — Lansdowne v UCD (AIB Lges 1)
Fri, 28th/ Sun, 30th — European Competitions Rd 2

Sat, 29th
- English Lges National 1 (8)
- English Lges National 2 (7)
- English Lges National 3 (6)
- English Lges (12s) (7)
- English Lges (10s) (6)
- Welsh Lges Prem, 1 (9)
- Welsh Lges all Divs 2+3 (9)
- Scottish Premiership 1-3 (10)
- Scottish Nat Lges 1-4 (8)
- AIB Lges 1-3 (3)

NOVEMBER 2005

Fri 4th — Welsh Lges Prem, 1 (10) (or midweek)

Fri, 4th/ Sun, 6th — Celtic League (7)

Sat, 5th
- English Senior Cup Rd 4
- English Lges National 3 (7)
- English Intermediate Cup and Junior Vase Rd 3
- Scottish Premiership 1-3 (11)
- AIB Lges 1-3 (4)

Sat, 12th — ENGLAND v AUSTRALIA (Twickenham)

	SCOTLAND v ARGENTINA (Murrayfield)
	WALES v FIJI (Cardiff)
	IRELAND v NEW ZEALAND (Dublin)
	FRANCE v SOUTH AFRICA (Paris)
	ITALY v TONGA (Rome)
	English Lges National 1 (9)
	English Lges National 2 (8)
	English Lges National 3 (8)
	English Lges (12s) (8)
	English Lges (10s) (7)
	Welsh Lges Prem,1 (11)
	Welsh Lges all Divs 2+3 (10)
	Scottish Premiership 1-3 (12)
	Scottish Nat Lges 1-4 (9)
Tue, 15th	Comb'd Services v Barbarians (TBA)
Fri, 18th	Welsh Lges Prem,1 (12) (or midweek)
Sat, 19th	ENGLAND v NEW ZEALAND (Twickenham)
	WALES v SOUTH AFRICA (Cardiff)
	IRELAND v AUSTRALIA (Dublin)
	FRANCE v TONGA (TBA)
	ITALY v ARGENTINA (Rome)
	English Lges National 1 (10)
	English Lges National 2 (9)
	English Lges National 3 (9)
	English Lges (12s) (9)
	Scottish Premiership 1-3 (13)
	Scottish Nat Lges 1-4 (10)
Sun, 20th	SCOTLAND v SAMOA (Murrayfield)
Fri, 25th	Welsh Lges Prem,1 (13) (or midweek)
Sat, 26th	ENGLAND v SAMOA (Twickenham)
	SCOTLAND v NEW ZEALAND (Murrayfield)
	WALES v AUSTRALIA (Cardiff)
	IRELAND v ROMANIA (Dublin)
	FRANCE v CANADA (Paris)
	ITALY v FIJI (Rome)
	English Senior Cup Rd 5
	English Intermediate Cup and Junior Vase Rd 4
	English Lges National 2 (10)
	English Lges National 3 (10)

DECEMBER 2005

Fri, 2nd/ Sun, 4th	Celtic League (8)
Sat, 3rd	BARBARIANS v SOUTH AFRICA (provisional; TBA)
	English Lges National 1-3 (11)
	English Lges (12s) (10)
	English Lges (10s) (8)

	Welsh Challenge Cup Rd 1
	Welsh Lges all Divs 2+3 (11)
	Scottish Cups Rd 1
	AIB Lges 1-3 (5)
Tue, 6th	OXFORD U v CAMBRIDGE U (Twickenham)
Fri, 9th/ Sun, 11th	European Competitions Rd 3
Sat, 10th	English Lges National 1-3 (12)
	English Lges (12s) (11)
	English Lges (10s) (9)
	Welsh Lges Prem,1 (14)
	Welsh Lges all Divs 2+3 (12)
	Scottish Premiership 1-3 (14)
	Scottish Nat Lges 1-4 (11)
	AIB Lges 1-3 (6)
Fri, 16th/ Sun, 18th	European Competitions Rd 4
Sat, 17th	English Lges National 2,3 (13)
	English Junior Vase Rd 5
	English Lges (12s) (12)
	Welsh Lges Prem,1 (15)
	Welsh Lges all Divs 2+3 (13)
	Scottish Premiership 1-3 (15)
	Scottish Nat Lges 1-4 (12)
Thu, 22nd/ Mon, 26th	Celtic League (9)
Sat, 24th	English Lges National 1 (13)
	Welsh Lges Prem,1 (16) (or Boxing Day)
Tue, 27th Wed, 28th or Thu, 29th	Blues v Dragons (Celtic Lge) Scarlets v Ospreys (Celtic Lge)
Sat, 31st	English Lges National 1 (14)
	Welsh Lges Prem,1 (17) (or Bank Holiday Monday)
Sat, 31st/ Mon, 2nd Jan	Celtic League (10)

JANUARY 2006

Sat, 7th	English Lges National 2,3 (14)
	English Senior Cup Rd 6
	English Lges (12s) (13)
	Engish Lges (10s) (10)
	Welsh Lges Prem,1 (18)
	Welsh Lges all Divs 2+3 (14)
	AIB Lges 1-3 (7)
	Scottish Premiership 1-3 (16)
	Scottish Nat Lges 1-4 (13)
Sat, 14th	English Lges National 1-3 (15)
	English Intermediate Cup Rd 5
	English Junior Vase Rd 6
	Welsh Challenge Cup Rd 2
	Welsh Lges all Divs 2+3 (15)
	AIB Lges 1-3 (8)
	Scottish Premiership 1-3 (17)
	Scottish Nat Lges 1-4 (14)
Sat, 21st	English Lges National 1-3 (16)
	English Lges (12s) (14)
	English Lges (10s) (11)
	Welsh Lges Prem,1 (19)

	Welsh Lges all Divs 2+3 (16)
	AIB Lges 1-3 (9)
	Scottish Cups Rd 2
Sat, 28th	English Senior Cup QF
	English Lges National 1-3 (17)
	English Lges (12s) (15)
	English Lges (10s) (12)
	Welsh Lges Prem,1 (20)
	Welsh Lges all Divs 2+3 (17)
	AIB Lges 1-3 (10)
	Scottish Premiership 1-3 (18)
	Scottish Nat Lges 1-4 (15)

FEBRUARY 2006

Fri, 3rd	England U21 v Wales U21
	Ireland U21 v Italy U21
	Scotland U21 v France U21
Sat, 4th	ENGLAND v WALES
	(Twickenham)
	IRELAND v ITALY (Dublin)
	English Intermediate Cup and
	Junior Vase QF
	Scottish Premiership 1-3 (19)
	Scottish Nat Lges 1-4 (16)
Sun, 5th	SCOTLAND v FRANCE
	(Murrayfield)
Fri, 10th	Italy U21 v England U21
	France U21 v Ireland U21
	Wales U21 v Scotland U21
Sat, 11th	ITALY v ENGLAND (Rome)
	FRANCE v IRELAND (Paris)
	English Lges National 1-3 (18)
	English Lges (12s) (16)
	English Lges (10s) (13)
	Welsh Lges Prem,1 (21)
	Welsh Lges all Divs 2+3 (18)
Sun, 12th	WALES v SCOTLAND (Cardiff)
Sat, 18th	English Lges National 1-3 (19)
	English Lges (12s) (17)
	English Lges (10s) (14)
	Welsh Challenge Cup Rd 3
	Welsh Lges Prem,1 (22)
	Welsh Lges all Divs 2+3 (19)
	AIB Lges 1-3 (11)
	Scottish Cups Rd 3
Fri, 24th	Scotland U21 v England U21
	France U21 v Italy U21
Sat, 25th	SCOTLAND v ENGLAND
	(Calcutta Cup; Murrayfield)
	FRANCE v ITALY (Paris)
	Ireland U21 v Wales U21
	English Lges National 1,3 (20)
	English Intermediate Cup and
	Junior Vase SF
	Scottish Premiership 1-3 (20)
Sun, 26th	IRELAND v WALES (Dublin)

MARCH 2006

Sat, 4th	English Senior Cup and
	Challenge Shield SF
	English Lges National 2 (20)

	English Lges National 3 (21)
	English Lges (12s) (18)
	English Lges (10s) (15)
	Welsh Lges Prem,1 (23)
	Welsh Lges all Divs 2+3 (20)
	AIB Lges 1-3 (12)
	Scottish Premiership 1-3 (21)
	Scottish Nat Lges 1-4 (17)
Fri, 10th	France U21 v England U21
	Ireland U21 v Scotland U21
	Wales U21 v Italy U21
Sat, 11th	WALES v ITALY (Cardiff)
	IRELAND v SCOTLAND (Dublin)
	English Lges National 1,2 (21)
	English Lges National 3 (22)
	English Lges (12s) (19)
	English Lges (10s) (16)
Sun, 12th	FRANCE v ENGLAND (Paris)
Wed, 15th	East Midlands v Barbarians
	(Northampton)
Thu, 16th	Leicester v Barbarians
	(provisional; Leicester)
Fri, 17th	England U21 v Ireland U21
	Wales U21 v Italy U21
	Welsh Lges Prem,1 (24)
	(or midweek)
Sat, 18th	ENGLAND v IRELAND
	(Twickenham)
	WALES v ITALY (Cardiff)
Sat, 25th	English Lges National 1,2 (22)
	English Lges National 3 (23)
	English Lges (12s) (20)
	English Lges (10s) (17)
	Welsh Lges Prem,1 (25)
	Welsh Lges all Divs 2+3 (21)
	AIB Lges 1-3 (13)
	Scottish Premiership 1-3 (22)
	Scottish Nat Lges 1-4 (18)

APRIL 2006

Sat, 1st	English Lges National 1,2 (23)
	English Lges National 3 (24)
	Welsh Challenge Cup QF
	Welsh Lges Prem,1 (26)
	Welsh Lges all Divs 2+3 (22)
	Scottish Cups QF
Sat, 1st and	European Competitions QF
Sun, 2nd	
Sat, 8th	English Senior Cup, Challenge
	Shield, Intermediate Cup and
	Junior Vase Finals
	(Twickenham)
	English Lges National 2 (24)
	English Lges National 3 (25)
	English Lges (12s) (21)
	English Lges (10s) (18)
	Welsh Lges Prem,1 (27)
	Welsh Lges all Divs 2+3 (23)
Sat, 15th	English Lges National 1 (24)
	Welsh Lges Prem,1 (28)
	Welsh Lges all Divs 2+3 (24)

	AIB Lges 1-3 (14)
	Scottish Cups SF
Sat, 22nd	English Lges National 1,2 (25)
	English Lges National 3 (26)
	English Lges (12s) (22)
	Welsh Challenge Cup SF
	Welsh Lges Prem,1 (29)
	Welsh Lges all Divs 2+3 (25)
Sat, 22nd and Sun, 23rd	European Competitions SF
Sat, 29th	English Lges National 1,2 (26)
	English County Championship Plate Rd 1
	Welsh Lges Prem,1 (30)
	Welsh Lges all Divs 2+3 (26)
	AIB Lges 1-3 (15)
	Scottish Finals Day (Murrayfield)

MAY 2006

Sat, 6th	Welsh Challenge Cup Final (Cardiff)
	Royal Navy v The Army (Twickenham)
	English County Championship Cup and Shield Rd 1
	English County Championship Plate Rd 2
	AIB Lges SF
Sat, 13th	English County Championship Cup and Shield Rd 2
	English County Championship Plate Rd 3
	AIB Lges Finals (Dublin)
Sat, 20th	Barbarians representative tour commences (provisional)
	English County Championship Cup and Shield Rd 3
	English County Championship Plate SF
Sat, 20th and Sun, 21st	European Competitions Finals
Midweek	Barbarians representative tour continues (provisional)
Sat, 27th	ENGLAND v BARBARIANS (provisional; Twickenham)
	English County Championship Cup, Shield and Plate Finals (Twickenham)

JUNE 2006

Sat, 10th	AUSTRALIA v IRELAND (TBA)
Sat, 17th	NEW ZEALAND v IRELAND (TBA)
Sat, 24th	NEW ZEALAND v IRELAND (TBA)

Rugby's charity supporting disadvantaged children and young people

Mission Statement

Wooden Spoon aims to enhance the quality and prospect of life for children and young persons in the United Kingdom who are presently disadvantaged either physically, mentally or socially

Charity Registration No: 326691